THE
REFLECTIONS ON CHRIS

Vincent MacNamara

The Truth in Love

REFLECTIONS ON CHRISTIAN MORALITY

GILL AND MACMILLAN

10383

Published in Ireland by
Gill and Macmillan Ltd
Goldenbridge
Dublin 8
with associated companies in
Auckland, Delhi, Gaborone, Hamburg, Harare,
Hong Kong, Johannesburg, Kuala Lumpur, Lagos, London,
Manzini, Melbourne, Mexico City, Nairobi,
New York, Singapore, Tokyo
© Vincent MacNamara, 1988
0 7171 1540 2
Print origination in Ireland by
Graphic Plan, Dublin
Printed in England by
Camelot Press, Southampton

CONTENTS

INTRODUCTION

I ALWAYS have a certain hesitation when I begin a series of lectures on Christian morality. It has to do with an awareness that my tradition has been very heavily moralistic and that this has had the effect of playing down other aspects of Christianity. It is a fair bet that if you asked one of us what it means to be a Roman Catholic you would get an answer about morality. You would probably be told that it is about doing something—loving one's neighbour or obeying the Church's teaching on moral matters. Some years ago the odds would have been even shorter: indeed you might have got an answer more removed from the centre of Christianity—a canonical or legal answer about going to Mass on Sundays or not eating meat on Fridays.

There is a danger of reducing Christianity to morality. I suspect that when we refer to the Catholic ethos we are thinking mainly in moral terms. Even when we say that people, perhaps young people, are losing the faith what is often meant is that they are rejecting certain moral teachings. My experience has been also that when the question is discussed whether or not there is a specific Christian morality someone invariably retorts, 'If there is not, what is the point of being a Christian?' Morality seems to be the most accessible and tangible part of our religion—as any preacher or congregation will tell you. We naturally and rightly expect religious people to be moral: if they are not, we incline to think that there is something phoney about them. But we may not be sure why we have this expectation. It helps, I think, to try to situate morality within our total Christian vision. It seems important to me, then, even in a book about Christian morality, to begin by saying that Christianity is centrally about faith in Jesus Christ.

Most of us have inherited our religion. We were born into it. Its way of life has been handed down to us. To be presented

1

with Catholicism ready made is to be presented with a complex form of life. There are so many bits and pieces to it, some crucial and others cultural, some central and others peripheral. There are bits of belief (truths about the Real Presence and the divinity of Christ), of ritual (rites of baptism and anointing), of canon law (the obligation of weekly Sunday Mass), of moral teaching (the Church's position on justice, abortion, divorce, war), of pious practices (the rosary, pilgrimages), of social organisation (parishes, Catholic schools), of historical accident (the primacy of the bishop of Rome rather than of Constantinople or London), of tradition (the special position of the Apostolic Nuncio to Ireland as dean of the diplomatic corps, the position of the Archbishop of Cashel as patron of the Gaelic Athletic Association). These are all jumbled together with perhaps no order or priority among them. It is important to be able to disentangle the different elements and weigh their significance: even in matters of doctrine Vatican II declared a hierarchy of truths. So I stress that Christianity is about faith

Faith in people is a kind of trust or confidence, a willingness to depend on them. We have faith in different people and depending on who and what they are our faith has different nuances—faith in doctors, mechanics, politicians, 'quacks', agricultural advisers, trainers of greyhounds. Some of these matters are of more importance than others. Religious faith is trust or dependence of a deep kind. It is trust in someone in relation to the most profound questions and concerns of life. Questions such as: who am I? where did I come from? what is my ultimate meaning? is there some kind of deity that made me? what kind? is it benign or hostile, interested or uninterested? can I be in contact with it? does my salvation or fulfilment relate to it? why do I die? is there life after death? Questions of ultimate concern.

We find that the New Testament message speaks to just such great areas. It is a message about God and his nature, about his initiative in our regard, about our meaning and destiny, about the centrality of Jesus Christ in world history, about love and mercy, about hope for a kingdom.[1] The acceptance of the great Christian stories—if it is a vital acceptance—gives our lives their fundamental character and direction: it shapes our understanding and vision, our sense of ourselves and our world, our meanings, our hopes, fears and aspirations. It informs our consciousness, affections and loyalties.

But what are we to do? It was a question which the first disciples asked also. It seems to me that we are first of all to 'Repent and believe the good news'. We are to allow the great stories to penetrate our lives. We are to let the conviction come true for us that reality (God) is accepting, that life is a gift, that God so loved the world that his Son was born of our flesh and lived amongst us, that life has point, that we are of more value than many sparrows, that our sins are forgiven, that we can have hope for the world. Before one arrives at the doing of morality there is the being and doing of faith attitudes. To believe in the Gospel of Jesus Christ, to share his faith, is, we are told, a conversion. But it is not only a moral conversion. It is a new way of seeing things. It gives us our basic philosophy of life, of who we are, where we come from, how we stand in the universe, where we are going.

All that is a sort of *caveat*. This book is about Christian morality or the moral dimension of faith. It helps to pause and advert to the fact of that moral dimension. We take it so much for granted. There is a twofold danger: that of reducing Christianity to morality and that of thinking that morality is tied to or arises only out of being a Christian. Christianity is a highly ethical religion. It does want to change our hearts, to change the world and to bring about a kingdom. We are rightly reminded today that faith should be performative: it is not an ideology that explains or justifies the present order. Moral concern for the neighbour and for the bringing about of a new world of justice and peace is the logic of faith in the Christian God. But it helps our grasp on things to recognise that religious faith and moral life are distinguishable ideas and that Christians can discuss intelligently how exactly their religion 'situates' morality. Faith is not solely about morals and moral life can obviously exist without faith. But there are several different kinds of connection and interdependence between faith and morals. For one who is religious, moral life takes on particular shades and contours. It has new and deep implications and assumes a new urgency.

We inherit a strong moral tradition. Christianity could be said to have been a bulwark of moral concern through the ages.

3

But it is a living tradition. It was formed by people like ourselves. We must be grateful for their wisdom, conservative of it. But it is necessary, increasingly necessary, for a Church to be an active, involved, articulate community. We have wisdom which earlier communities did not have and could not have had. We can see their errors and prejudices—and the reasons for them—as future generations will see ours. We have a different consciousness and cultural awareness. We have problems which they did not face. We have an ongoing responsibility then, all of us, to explore moral issues. It is in the whole community that the Spirit resides and it is to the whole community that the mission of Christ is entrusted. Unless the whole community is involved there is a rejection of wisdom, a failure to listen to what the Spirit is saying to the Church.

It is important then that all should feel that they can and should contribute to the discussion of moral issues and to the elaboration of positions. This book is intended as an encouragement, to help people to share in the making of theology, to make more available some of the language and concepts of morality and some of the range of views among Catholic theologians. It is written from within the perspective of the Roman Catholic Church but I know that some of its concerns are shared by many of the Churches: when I refer to the Church I intend it in this limited sense. It is a book about fundamental aspects of morality. People find it easier perhaps to consider particular topics—to head into argument about the morality of justice, divorce, abortion etc. These are concrete issues. Fundamentals are more basic and abstract. And yet unless one tackles them one is building a house on sand: one is likely to be merely asserting positions rather than arguing for them.

This then is an invitation to get beneath the individual issues and to examine the broad concepts of moral life: I have called the chapters 'reflections'; I intend them to be relatively self-contained but I hope that there is a forward movement in the book. We need to know what we are talking about when we refer to the moral or ethical dimension of life (Chapter 1)—I am using the words interchangeably although they do have technical uses. We can argue that morality is autonomous but then we must ask how it is to be referred to God and what is the

4

relation between the ideas and language of morality—good, bad, right, wrong, obligation—and the language of the Christian message—grace, salvation, sin, damnation (Chapter 2). We need to study our moral tradition in our sacred books (the Bible), to ask in what sense it is authoritative for us and to consider the wider question of the bearing of faith on the content of morality (Chapter 3). We can ask if there is some central theme of the Christian moral tradition—most people plump immediately for love (agape). Is it the source of our values and rules and what are the implications for saying so: or are there better theories; what do we mean by the natural law on which our tradition depends so much? (Chapters 4, 5). How adequate are moral statements anyway: can they be absolute and in what sense? (Chapter 7) How useful it is to propose morally right theories or rules: how likely are we to appreciate them; how well can we respond? (Chapter 6). What is our individual responsibility in conscience: what does 'following conscience' mean or an 'informed conscience'? (Chapter 8). What are we to make of our moral weakness and failure: what is the Christian perspective on them? (Chapter 9, Epilogue).

1

APPROACHING CHRISTIAN MORALITY

ONE could begin this study by considering the history of morality within our Judaeo-Christian tradition and there might be good reasons for such an approach. But it seems best first to determine in some fashion the particular area of Christianity that concerns us: that of morality. So I propose that we try to isolate the word 'morality' in 'Christian morality' and to reflect on what we mean by it. We all know a fair bit about morality so we should feel reasonably comfortable with the subject. It is not as if we were heading into unknown territory. We feel the call to be moral—fair, just, caring, unselfish, forgiving etc.—and are often unhappy that we are not as good as we might be. We are well aware of making distinctions between acts which we call right or good and the opposite which we call wrong or bad. Our conversations and newspapers witness to such concerns: 'There is no honesty today'/'She is a very upright person'/'He will give you a fair deal'/'I find it hard to forgive him the wrong he did me'/'He treated her very badly'/'Human life is sacred'/'Survey shows decline in moral standards'/'Irish people are racist'/'Ireland responds generously to distress'/'There is a right to divorce'/'Human rights denied in South Africa'.

We think of morality primarily as applying to acts. But a little reflection shows us that we refer it also to intentions, dispositions, desires and character. And we use different forms of moral language: consider the difference between 'Do not steal'/'She is a very honourable person'/'Honesty is an important virtue today'. We not only make these distinctions between one kind of behaviour and another. We recognise that the statements are not merely factual or neutral statements: they commit us in some way. It is not like saying that something is white or round. When we say that a piece of behaviour is immoral we recognise that it is to be avoided. When we acknowledge that a course of action is right we mean that it is commendable, that its pursuit by ourselves or others is worthy of praise: we recognise some kind of call to live in that way. There is something prescriptive in our understanding of morality, some sense of obligation or claim on us. Whether we will follow what we recognise to be the moral way or not is, of course, another matter altogether.

This, I suppose, is our unreflective experience. It is what we have picked up as we have gone through life. For most of us it is very much part of our tradition and especially of our religion. But however prominent moral considerations might be in our consciousness we may find, if we question ourselves, that we are not too clear about what we mean by this morality talk. We are not clear about where morality comes from, about what it means to call (or why we call) a particular piece of behaviour right or good, and about what we mean by saying that the right ought to be done and the wrong avoided.

Let us spell that out. (a) We have trouble about the source of morality, in particular about whether it comes from God—from the Ten Commandments perhaps—and about how our moral conduct relates us to him. (b) We have trouble about our criterion for saying what kind of conduct is acceptable or not. (It may well be that we have never examined our moral positions, that we have a lopsided morality, a Victorian morality or a bourgeois morality, or that what passes for morality in our lives is really parental directives.) It is this problem of determining what is right and wrong that interests people almost exclusively about morality. But we need to go beyond particular issues to ask ourselves why we say and how we know (who tells us) that things are right or wrong. And we need to go beyond that again to ask what we mean by the whole business of calling acts right and wrong. That is, we must ask ourselves not only what is right and wrong but what the words 'right' and 'wrong' mean for us and why we use them. What would you say? You may hold a set of moral principles: murder/abortion/stealing/lying are wrong. What do you mean by the 'wrong' bit? (c) We have trouble with the prescriptive element, with what we might refer to as moral obligation, with *why* we must do right and avoid wrong. We sometimes refer to morality as a law, perhaps as the law of God. Is it from God that morality gets its binding force?

We have trouble, I think, nailing down the moral point of view. That there is such a point of view we have no doubt. We need the language of morality and most of us would regard it as entirely natural to have recourse to the kind of judgment that we label as moral. We cannot say what we want to say about ourselves and others, we cannot describe how life presents itself to us, without its language and concepts. So deeply engrained in us is this dimension of experience that it would be difficult for us to live a day without the whole tissue of language of 'right', 'wrong', 'good', 'bad', 'duty', 'obligation', 'ought', 'praise' and 'blame', as well as much moral language of a softer kind. This is not to say that we are always in the area of morality when we use such words, but we often are. We say 'he ought to be here any minute', 'he should have taken a 7 iron', 'he is a good philosopher'. These we know are not about morality. But compare 'he ought to treat his wife better', 'he should not kill', 'he is a good man'. These are about morality. It is true that there are fuzzy edges around the area of morality, some points at which we are not sure whether we are making moral judgments or perhaps judgments about manners or good taste. But by and large we know when we are talking morality and when we are not. It is an area that has a high degree of determinateness.

In making moral statements we are not merely expressing our tastes: they are not in the same category as statements that a person likes cucumber or the Connemara landscape or tweeds or heavy rock. It is perfectly alright for you to like one thing and for me to like another. Such things do not greatly matter: there is no right and wrong or true and false about them. But there are areas of living in which it matters a great deal what we value and do—issues of one's right to life, of justice, of respect for others i.e. moral issues. We are not prepared to say that in making these statements we are merely expressing a subjective view of desirable human behaviour and that it is perfectly fine for another to hold and act on the opposite point of view. We believe that there is an objectivity about our statements, like for example, 'torture is wrong'. If we hold this position we do not regard others as rationally justified in holding the opposite: we do not mean that torture is wrong for us but may

8

be right for them. We believe that there is a truth to be discovered here, a truth for living that is as rigorous as truth in any other area and that the judgments we are making are somehow founded in the natures and relations of things. We would expect to be able to give reasons of some kind for our positions, to justify them. Or at least we feel that they are justifiable, that an expert could in some sense demonstrate the reasonableness of them.

If we were asked to give some elementary account of this experience we might come up with a variety of suggestions. There would possibly emerge ideas of fairness, impartiality, respect for self and others, concern for human flourishing, a vision of a good society, a recognition that there is a kind of life that fits our rational nature. They are different but related ideas. They are all in some sense about persons in community. So even at this stage we can mark down that morality is not a series of unexplained and arbitrary commands and prohibitions coming from heaven only knows where. It arises rather as the human community's awareness of the claims and demands of interrelatedness. All of morality in the end is about this. It is the search for the acts, attitudes, dispositions—and more fundamentally perhaps the virtues and institutions—that make for successful being with others.

This moral strand of experience is a powerful and compelling one. It makes insistent demands and while it can be ignored it is only with difficulty that it can be entirely quelled or silenced. There is something deep in us that wants to be moral, that desires goodness, and it is well to remember this. Not to realise this is to fail to understand oneself. We will argue later that listening to the moral thrust is listening to what we most deeply desire. But to call attention to this alone would be to give a false picture. The intriguing thing is that it appears in the midst of much else. We are centres of so much energy and not all of it points unerringly in the moral direction. We do not always listen to the call of morality because we do not want only to be moral beings. We want to be and do and express ourselves in many other ways. We have such a restless urge to create our own identities, our egos, to satisfy fundamental needs and desires, to bond and to be separate, to be loved and to be independent. We experience these drives as powerful forces within us—powerful and also subtle because we seek to achieve the ends or objects of our energy in all kinds of guises and camouflages, even under the guise of virtue, goodness and holiness. So, as each of us knows, there is an energy in us that does not necessarily take account of fairness, impartiality or respect for others. We beg, flatter, threaten, manipulate, love, hate, compete, fight and sometimes kill to satisfy our insistent needs.

There seems to be a conflict between our thrust towards morality and the rest of our energies. Or perhaps it is that we are disjointed, that we have not got our act together. We have not integrated our energies in the service of our deepest and most complete desires, of whole human living. Each of us experiences the problem uniquely because each is the history of how he/she has coped through the years with the demands of these energies: the particular shape and momentum which they have in our lives is the legacy of that history. We are responsible for it only in part. None of us has been invited to choose the terrain of his/her life's struggle. It has been basically staked out by the evolutionary process: we are at the same time vegetative, animal, human—half-beast, half-angel. It has been further determined by our genetic code, our parents, our early experiences. And, as we shall see, it has been affected by how we have lived our lives until now. But one way or another we have to live with ourselves: we have to include all this in our understanding of our (moral) selves and in our efforts to achieve wholeness and harmony.

It would be interesting to discover what kind of image we have of this. We may see ourselves as a jumble of conflicting urges and energies. Many people see a clear duality, a division in themselves, a good and bad self: they plug into St Paul's experience of two laws within him, one the source of good actions and the other apparently urging him towards what is wrong (Rom. 7). Others see morality as imposed on them from outside, something foreign to them, to which they consent with their heads but which does not touch their hearts: it enables them to keep their altogether wayward energies in check—but only just. Religious upbringing may have encouraged us to see things in this way. Religion or philosophy does play quite a part. Its basic metaphysic or world-view colours our thinking on such related issues as: am I good; is creation/human nature good; are body, flesh, matter, eros

10

good and to be trusted; what is my most fundamental energy; is morality in harmony with my being and desires or is it anti-life; is there evil in me—and in what way; am I split; can I be moral; what if I cannot; do I need 'outside' help; is there evil in the world—a devil 'who wanders around the world seeking the ruin of souls'? Our stance—and it may be unreflective—on such issues shapes our sense of ourselves and our moral lives. Our religious tradition in the main has had a predominant distrust of desire and instinct: they were to be curbed by grace and sacrament; 'agere contra' was the watchword.

It is well to be realistic about our situation. On the one hand there is no point in suggesting that each of us is a pure and limpid fountain of moral striving. On the other we have to recognise that our instincts and energies are the source of our being and doing: without them we would not survive, create or relate. We might think of ourselves perhaps as trying to fashion or allowing to emerge out of the totality of our energies a personality or character that corresponds to our deepest desires. These, I think, are about some vision of a life of harmonious being-with-others. I think we all have in our hearts a kind of person we would like to be, an ideal self. If we were asked to write our ideal obituary it is very likely that we would include all the noblest and most other-regarding virtues. It is what we want. It is part of us. It is an energy in us. It is important then to recognise that there is a deep desire in us for moral living, for goodness. If our image of ourselves does not include this we have got it wrong and we may go through life with a distorted view of and feel about ourselves.

TWO ELEMENTS

(a) *Judgment about Good and Bad Activity*

Let us pursue further this business of morality. Two different but related points have emerged already. The first is that we label certain kinds of activity as right or good. The second is that we know that we ought to do what is right and avoid what is wrong: there is within our experience a sense of—of what? Some would say of law or obligation to act in a certain way, others of a tension towards one's potential being, others of the call of a value that is worth pursuing, others of the sense of the fittingness of a way of life, of the flourishing it brings.

11

What do we mean by referring to activity as right or good? Take the word 'good'. 'This is a good car'/'She is a good teacher'. 'Good' talk is a particular kind of talk. It is not as easy as talk about the size or weight or colour of things. It is sometimes referred to as value language—as against fact language. It involves more discussion and seems to have criteria built into it in a way that fact language does not. It is so much easier to say that this car is 10′ long or that this teacher is 5′5″ or blonde or slim or French. It is possible to reach agreement on such matters in a way that is not possible with 'good'. It is not easy to agree about a good car or teacher or cook or lawn-mower or sculptor or pianist. People will argue and disagree about such matters. If we seek to resolve the disagreement perhaps the best we can do is to ask ourselves what cars or lawn-mowers or teachers or cooks or artists are meant to do—and we might have trouble with 'meant to'.

We are in the same general area of value-language when we say that someone performed a good act or has a good character, but we have introduced a new dimension. Because we recognise that one can be a good teacher or cook or artist—or an expert on prayer or religion—without being a person of good character. One can be very developed and complete (and perhaps then 'good') at the one level but not at the other. Indeed one may fail at the level of morality precisely in the effort to become good at a different level—it is not uncommon that one develops a talent or profession and in the process neglects his/her family. Of course one may be a good teacher and a bad cook or a good pianist and a hopeless golfer: we all know that and nobody worries about it. Few will criticise a person who neglects the pursuit of excellence in cooking or games. But it is a different matter with good character or good action. The judgment that someone is good as a person or has a good character is one of much deeper significance. Most of us recognise in our better moments that it is this judgment that really matters, and we are alarmed if someone sees no distinction between concern for games or gardening and that for the lives of refugees faced with starvation. The simple searing judgment that one is or is not a good person is not in the same category as judgments about other kinds of achievement. (It is the kind of judgment that one often hears at funerals—'she was a decent woman'—when other apparently less significant

church going

12

considerations fade into the background.) Of course if people disagree about good lawn-mowers or cooks or artists they will disagree even more profoundly and perhaps more strongly about good living, and much of the history of ethical writing has been about this disagreement and the reasons for it. But they will largely agree that there *is* a judgment of a moral kind to be made, that there is something called moral living and moral character.

This moral awareness is a fact of life and an abiding fact in our history and literature. In all cultures and in all times men and women have recognized this level of assessment. They may differ about what is right and wrong. But they have no doubt that some kinds of act and purposes etc. are right and the opposite wrong. In a particular culture it may be accepted that a man has ten wives. (They stand in a particular relationship to him and he to them and both sides to all others in the society: this establishes norms which have significance in the society, which all are expected to adhere to and the violation of which may bring sanction.)

It is inspiring to find Plato say that it is better to suffer wrong than to cause it. (Many have remarked on the curious asymmetry involved here which reaches its highest point in the teaching of the New Testament that we should even be prepared to lay down our lives for others.) Aristotle puzzles about the fact that the action which we know to be right and fitting for us does not always bring reward. There is the famous statement of Cicero that there is a moral law in us from which neither Senate nor people can dispense us and to deny which is to flee from ourselves and go against our nature. And perhaps the even more famous statement of Sophocles' Antigone that she had a moral responsibility towards her dead brother which no State law or custom could override.

(b) A sense of Obligation
But why should we *do* what we call 'right' or 'good'? How does the prescriptive idea—the sense of obligation, call, or fittingness get into these notions? Why should we do what very often we do not like doing or what does not appear to be to our advantage? You will hear people say when some piece of sharp practice is suggested to them, 'I could not do that' when it is obvious at another level that they can do it. There is nothing

13

stopping them from doing it. Well, nothing physical. But is there something? I remember one evening walking through the botanic gardens of a city where I was giving a course on morality: a mother and child came towards me and the mother said to the frolicking child, 'You cannot pick the flowers, everyone would want to pick the flowers'. It was a useful starting point for a lecture next morning: it seemed to me that she was giving expression to moral experience and even revealing her own moral theory. What does 'cannot' or 'could not' signify? What does the language of 'ought' or 'should' mean or where does it come from? It is a useful exercise to ask ourselves such questions: it forces us to sharpen our ideas about morality.

Some Christians collapse the whole of morality into religion. They operate with the idea that it was God who gave us our moral rules. And since morality has come from God, who is creator and Lord of all things, they have a clear notion of moral obligation: God has set out the way of life which we must follow; he has ordered us to obey it; he will reward us with heaven if we do so and punish us in hell if we do not. I find that if you push people a bit about morality or its source they almost invariably refer it back to God—probably to the Ten Commandments. This is rock bottom for them.

> Mosaic imperatives bang home like rivets;
> God is a foreman with certain definite views
> Who orders life in shifts of work and leisure.
>   (Seamus Heaney, *Death of a Naturalist*)

This amounts to saying that God decided some time in the past what is right and wrong, that indeed the very meaning of the word 'wrong' is 'prohibited by God'. Others have some sense that the right/wrong distinction is independent of God and somehow rooted in the natures of things: God has given directives about morality, they say, but it is only to confirm and clarify matters. Still others think of God mainly in terms of the force of morality, of obligation. They say that morality is rooted in the natures of things and may say that we are left by God to work out the details of right and wrong but that we are to do the right and avoid the wrong because God wills this—it is the law of God that we do so. This is what they mean by 'ought' or 'should' in moral contexts: this is *why* we must do

14

the right and avoid the wrong. God, for them, is the source of moral obligation.

It is difficult for Christians to separate their morality from their religion. In a sense they are right: if one is a believer one's morality will be affected in various ways, as we shall see. I will argue later that we all do morality in some context: Christians do it in theirs. But the best service we can do to Christian morality may well be to distinguish our moral from our religious experience. There are many who are entirely convinced of the validity of the distinction of right and wrong and who are deeply conscious of the need to abide by it but who do not believe in God. This comes as a surprise to some Christians: you will hear them say, 'they are very good people although they do not go anywhere (i.e. to any Church)'. Non-believers are often very sensitively moral people—even to put it like this is to suggest some surprise. There is no reason why they should not be. But we have become so accustomed to experiencing morality in a religious context and to having Churches make statements about it that we behave as if somehow they had ownership of it or a monopoly of it or special insight into it. Not only do unbelievers live well but some of the most important movements for moral progress have been initiated and inspired by those who were not Christian or were even anti-Christian. So too some of the best work in the understanding of morality has come from un-believers. It is important for Christians to advert to that. It looks entirely obvious. But morality has become so sub-ordinated to our religious tradition that the point needs to be made. So I have insisted that we try to make distinctions between faith and morals.

MORALITY A HUMAN INSTITUTION

This has been leading to the suggestion that we see morality as a human institution, as something that arises spontaneously out of our human situation. It might help to ground it if we referred to it as the moral fact. It is a fact of life that as we become aware of life together in community certain basic directions of action suggest themselves—with regard to the meaning and dignity of the individual, to human welfare, to fairness and impartiality, to the creation of a just society. We

15

come to realise that being true to ourselves as persons involves us in response to such considerations, that our selfhood becomes possible in our relations with others. This recognition of the inescapable claim of such values as truth, life, justice, equality and fraternity has been one of the greatest and most precious insights of the human spirit.

In doing morality, then, (and in trying to teach or defend it) we are concerning ourselves with one of the great questions of the human race i.e. how is the human person to live? Which is also the question: what does it mean to be a person? It has been a concern of human kind from the beginning. It is not a question that we make so much as a question that we find within ourselves and to which we must attend if we are to be at peace. It makes a claim on us: we cannot manipulate it easily; in a sense it is greater than we are. It is sometimes said that it has a sacred character about it, that it is religious. I take that to mean that it is perceived and experienced as something of utmost importance and dignity, something to which we must attend or pay the price of knowing that we have not been true to ourselves. We cherish and reflect on certain classic statements of it in philosophy and in literature because we find that certain writers have successfully caught and illuminated it for us.

It is important then to recognise this moral experience in ourselves and others. Even for Christians it is a useful starting point. To see it in this perspective may be some relief, indeed, especially for those who teach morality. One sometimes feels burdened by the task of teaching as if somehow the Church had made morality or was responsible for it. It is not Christianity that has made morality, not the Church, not even God, except in the sense that he has made us. It is even more fundamental, more basically human than that. So if we are teachers we should not feel that we are importing morality into the lives of others. It is there already in some sense: what we are trying to do is to help people to understand themselves. Our role is to awaken and encourage their own questions about how the human being is to live. It is a question that is native to all of us, and no one can afford to belittle it or treat it lightly. We can make contact with it even in those who appear to rebel against morality. Because while they may reject particular statements of it they would insist that they be treated rightly. For example, young people in school are quick to sense favouritism: they are

16

sensitive about being bullied or treated harshly; they may even insist that morality should not be rammed down their throats. They are saying in their own fashion that there is a way for people to live together. Perhaps we can build on that.

What I am talking about here, obviously, is the basis or source of morality. The fuller implications of living together are to be worked out. Some of them are easy to come by: there should be respect for truth and life, equality before the law, freedom of conscience, provision for the young and defenceless. Others are more difficult: is violent revolution legitimate in situations of unjust rule; are government cut-backs unfairly affecting the disadvantaged; is the zygote to be treated with the same respect as one's next door neighbour; how is one to act in a situation where mother and child will die if one does nothing? Nobody doubts that there will be differences about such details. But long before that stage is reached there can be some agreement on what morality is all about and on the original source of principles. At this level at least we can be seen to make sense to people.

THE AUTONOMY OF MORALITY

I am suggesting that morality has a certain autonomy. By this I mean that it makes its own demand: you could say that one should be moral because one should be moral. One does not need to know God before becoming aware of moral distinctions or moral demands: morality does not immediately need religion. It is true that a religious tradition, like any other group, may have arrived at certain conclusions about how one is to be moral, may give support to the whole enterprise of morality, may have its own understanding of the ultimate significance of it. But even if religion is abandoned, a person is still left with the morality question unless being human is also to be abandoned. Morality has been so dominated by religion that young people especially seem to think that because they have given up faith they are entitled to give up morality. This is to misunderstand its origin. You might say that if there were no God there would be no morality because we would not exist. That is true. But God is not the author of the principles of morality. Morality is a human thing. What God asks of us is that we listen to ourselves, listen to the moral call within us.

Neither does morality depend on reward. Many fine moral people who do not believe in God or in heaven do believe in being moral. For them virtue is its own reward i.e. the knowledge that they are living in the way in which they believe human beings should live. They are not slow to point out that if they live well it is because they believe in the value and dignity of the other and not simply because someone has told them to do so or because they hope for any reward. Some even accuse Christian morality of being anti-morality because it is so closely linked to reward in the popular consciousness. Christians, they say, are not really interested in morality but only in themselves—in saving their souls. They have a point. Morality makes its own demand: it appeals to us to recognise that there is a truth for doing, that there is a humanising way of living together, that there is a form of genuine society to be created. To collapse morality into religion, to attribute its genesis to a decree of God is to make a true appreciation of it difficult. If someone is led to believe that morality has only to do with being a Christian or that it is something that one accepts if one wishes to ensure future happiness, then it has been devalued. It is easy to have such notions in a religious morality.

Morality therefore is independent of the Churches. It is a human experience and institution which Churches must rather acknowledge. It may be important to the religious life of Churches. They may think they are good at it or know a lot about it or protect it. (There will be those, of course, who will dispute such claims.) They may demand it from their members. But they do not have a monopoly of it. They do not make morality and cannot in any sense make things right or wrong. They have to *find out* what is right or wrong. They can give their opinion on such matters. But as in every other area of life the value of their opinion depends on their competence, their diligence and their honesty. Things are never right or wrong because somebody says so, but because of the way we are in the world. So the fact that a Church makes statements about war or rights or revolution or marriage does not affect the morality of such actions. They are either right or wrong in themselves. Neither can the Churches afford to ignore the fact that there are a great many honourable and intelligent non-Christians who are just as concerned about moral issues as they are. They ought perhaps to see their role as that of sharing with all people of goodwill the struggle to discover what is best for the human community, what is the good society. Their concern for morality should be a passion for the welfare of society and not just a defence of established positions.

THE HUMAN SEARCH FOR MORALITY

It helps, I think, to see morality as the result of the great search of the human race from the beginning. It is a continuing search: there is room for and need for development through the ages. Society once regarded slavery as acceptable. Plato, Aristotle and probably St Paul would have told you that it was part of the natural law that some are born slaves and some free. It took the human race a long time to break out of that. Society once regarded women as inferior and to some extent it still does: we are only slowly and painfully coming to a realisation of the implications of seeing all as equal. Child labour and laissez faire capitalism, especially in international trade, were once thought to be normal but not anymore. My own country has seen a welcome—at least I think it is welcome—development of thinking about our moral obligation to the handicapped, the travellers, homosexuals, those born out of wedlock, prisoners, etc. We once regarded capital punishment as moral. Well, is it? Our society seems to be divided about it. How many more areas do we have to develop? We are now more concerned about ecological ethics and one finds books about animal rights. The frontiers of morality are being pushed out. One could think of the whole of humanity slowly and painfully trying to work out over the ages what it means to live satisfactorily together. In that sense it is true to say that we make our morality. At least we discover it. But 'discovery' here is not like finding something ready-made. We have to work at it, to figure things out.

Who is to say, people often ask. Who is to say whether a particular position is an instance of development or the opposite? You could consult your tradition or your elders. But how do they know? One often gets the reply that the Church will tell us. But official Church authorities make statements only about a few crucial issues. For most of the thousand and one everyday moral situations there is no Church teaching. We have to do the best we can. There is nobody to go to, at least nobody

19

except ourselves and our fellow human beings. Aristotle would have told you to go to the wise person and that surely is good advice. Some find this difficult. They find it difficult to accept that moral knowledge depends on our fallible minds and the idea of change is hard to take. But that is how it is. It is no more likely that we will have certainty about the moral question than about anything else—psychology or philosophy or medicine for example. We do not know the answers to many of the problems in these areas: why should we expect to know them about morality? There are several critical areas of faith in which we might have liked more certainty. We know so little about God—in fact we seem to be less bold in making statements about Him than we were a few decades ago. We go on searching in all the major areas of Christology. We know next to nothing about our future condition, about life after death. And yet we manage. In morality we have to manage as best we can also. We have to find the best answers we can for ourselves and our children. That is all we can hope for.

With regard to this very issue there seems to be a division between those who, while appreciating the value of the past and the need to conserve, still see society as in a continuing state of search and discovery—in the area of morals as in every other area—and those who see morality as something that is settled, that has been decided by God and given to the Churches to promote and defend. For the second group questions about morality are non-questions: all has been determined. Morality is perhaps seen as a matter of loyalty to one's Church and the questioning of it is regarded as at least a carelessness about one's heritage and at worst an undermining of the order of one's Church and society. But morality is about something more fundamental than loyalty. It is about truth, the truth of living together in love, and that is independent of the Churches. The natural law tradition is the quintessence of this. Essentially it has said that things are right or wrong because of their nature, not because the law of the land says so and not because religion says so. There is an independence to the institution of morality.

MISINTERPRETATIONS

To concentrate on the inner character of morality in this way is to invite misinterpretation. So I had better say what I do *not* mean. I do not mean that everybody simply makes up his/her own mind without reference to community or tradition. One learns morality in a community as one learns everything else: the moral tradition is part of the total wisdom of the community which is being handed on. I do not mean that one has to wait until a person 'sees' and accepts a moral position interiorly: morality can be taught and at some stage in a child's life perhaps one should insist. Neither do I mean that all are equally good at working out the requirements of morality or equally open to it. We have in the community experts in the science of morality (as in any other science) and experts in living it. Nor do I mean that everything is fine provided you think that what you are doing is right: there is a truth to be discovered here as elsewhere and it is important for the individual and for the community that it be discovered. I therefore do not mean that one solution to a moral question is as good as another or one moral system as good as another. I do not mean that a Christian does or thinks about morality exactly like a humanist: it will be as a Christian and out of the Christian vision of life that he/she will work out the details of morality—just as a Marxist or atheist will do it from his/hers. A Christian will see morality as, in some sense, the law of God. He/she will have religious reasons for being moral that the humanist has not. His/her morality will be significant for a relationship with God. And it may be that a specific content to Christian morality will be found.

I have talked about morality as a general term and have said that it is found in all ages and cultures. But that may be to oversimplify. I have no doubt that there are quite different notions about it. I do not mean only about what is right and wrong but about how things come to be right and wrong and what these terms mean. Ask yourself what would someone in an Eastern culture mean by morality, or someone, say, in an African animist culture, or a person who has always lived in deprived circumstances in the slums of a great city, or an agnostic Oxbridge don. We gather them all under the one umbrella of morality, but it may be that there is only a very general family resemblance between their ideas. It may be that the only thing that morality has in common from one society to another is that rules for living are generally accepted in the society, that they are in some way enforced (at least by public opinion) and that in relation to other rules they are considered to be over-riding. In the following chapters my concern is with general Western culture—and indeed within that one will find a variety of notions— and especially with communities who interpret their lives religiously in Jesus Christ.

My interest so far has been to establish some preliminary points about the basic meaning and source of morality. I have been trying to winkle out what ideas we have about it. We all have a kind of unreflective morality. To ask ourselves questions is to try to become more aware, more conscious of our processes, and that can only be good. The problem still remains of finding the right answers to the question of how we should live. But my hope is that we would realise that the whole paraphernalia—the whole panoply of values, rules, commandments, as well as the explorations of meta-ethics—is an attempt to understand the experience and spell out its implications. For the individual the task of moral life is to listen to the experience and grow in openness to it, to do the truth in love. For the community the task is to encourage the individual to interpret this experience aright and to be able to respond to it. It is an educative task. It is a worthy vocation.

THE CONTEXT OF CHRISTIAN MORALITY: MORALITY AND GOD

TO say that morality is a human phenomenon raises questions for Christians. This is understandable. Christians think of morality in a religious context. For many of them God and their relation to God are the point of morality: one sometimes finds the notion that if there were no God there would be no morality and no moral obligation. This link of morality and God appears widely in popular religious practice. Consider, for example, what happens in confession. The penitent comes to the priest and confesses that he/she has perhaps damaged a neighbour's property. This is something that is a human fault, a moral failure—it is something for which any atheist might reproach himself/herself. But both priest and penitent begin immediately to talk about God. The penitent refers to what he/she has done as a sin and asks God for pardon: the priest gives assurance that God does indeed grant pardon. For many penitents the crucial thing about their moral failure is whether God has indeed pardoned them—whether, as we say, their sins have been wiped away. Our morality is clearly tied up with God. But how or why we make this link is worth examining. Is it, for example, that God forbade us to destroy the property of others and made the respecting of his laws the condition of union with him? What has happened here to the autonomy of morality?

There seems to be a question here about how we relate two great and distinguishable areas of experience—the areas of morality and religion. Morality, we have argued, is an autonomous human experience, in particular one that is independent of religion. It has to do with a perception about the needs of our interpersonal and social lives. Religion has to do with our ultimate concern about the meaning of ourselves and our lives—particularly our interpretation of the deity and our relations with him, her, it or them. What is in question here is the the manner in which we bring together these two relatively independent areas of our experience. We Christians all have, consciously or unconsciously, some scheme by which we hold together our notions of deity, moral life and salvation.

The text books of moral theology which were in use up to recently and the catechisms on which at least the older generation were trained had very clear ideas about all of this. They had, as we shall see, a very tight system in which the three factors—God, morality, union with God (heaven/hell) were locked together. This tight system has broken down somewhat and it is a matter of opinion whether that is a good thing or not. You often hear it said nowadays that there is no sense of sin any more or that young people have lost the sense of sin. One might wonder just what is meant here: that they have no morals? that they have no fear of God? that they think of God differently? that morality has a different significance for their relations with God?

THE TEN COMMANDMENTS

Our tradition and our sacred books certainly put morality firmly in a God context, so much so that it is difficult for us now to think of it in any other context. Probably the decisive event in the moral consciousness of the Judaeo-Christian people has been the Bible story of the giving of the Decalogue. The Bible says that Moses went to meet God who gave him the Decalogue which was to be the moral code of his people. Some readers will remember the picture in the old Bible history of Moses coming down from the mountain with two chunks of stone on which the commandments were carved. The Bible surrounded the event with impressive imagery of fire and smoke which our Bible history tried to capture. This dramatic scene has burned itself into our consciousness and has in large part determined our notion of morality and its associations. It certainly *looks* like the giving of morality by God, the imposition of it with his authority and the threat of a divine sanction for refusal to observe it.

But we have to be careful how we read a story such as that of Moses. The very least that is to be said about biblical inter-

24

pretation is that not everything in the Bible is to be taken literally. We know, for example, that we are not to accept literally the story of creation, or of Adam and Eve or of Jonah or even some of the detail of the infancy narratives. They were written for our instruction and have a message for us. The question is: what message? We are getting into a big question here about the authority of the Bible in moral matters which will concern us later. But at least we can recognise that we do not need to accept literally the account of the giving of the law to Moses. There are good reasons for thinking that the commandments were not 'handed down' in the fashion described in the Bible story.

We know from internal evidence that the morality of the actual versions of the Decalogue which we now have is most likely to have come from a later period in the history of Israel, from that of the prophets, and to have been written back into the stories about Moses by a later generation. However, it is probable that an earlier, skeletal version of the Decalogue does go back to the time of Moses. Some scholars believe they can reconstruct this. The Decalogue is an element in a covenant or treaty between God and his people. What is interesting and what suggests that an early form of the Decalogue can be attributed to Moses is that the basic form of treaty which we find in the Decalogue event is also found in extra-biblical literature that is contemporaneous with Moses. But we also know from the same literature that the neighbours of the Jews had moral codes of similar content. There was no need for a special revelation from God to Moses. What we have in the Decalogue is an elementary code of conduct that was necessary for the survival of a society. Most societies find it necessary to produce some such code and most have shown themselves perfectly capable of doing so. Morality is simply an inescapable element of living together in society.

Why then is the story of Moses' acceptance of the Decalogue recounted in the Bible? Moses did, in the providence of God, contribute something very important to the religious and moral development of his people and to the tradition which we inherit. He showed them that as a people of God they were to be a moral people. The God of Moses was not an evil, capricious God. He was not to be identified with the gods of the pagans and their strange orgies. He was a good God, a moral being,

with a care for his people and a purpose in their history. They too were to live moral lives: the fact that they were the chosen people of God did not absolve them from that but rather accentuated it. So their religion was to be a moral religion: they could not please God or be his people if they were not moral. And their morality was to be religious. Living morally or failing to do so, listening to their native moral call or rejecting it, was not some neutral affair. It involved them with God. So that morality was inescapable for them and could be said to be the law of God. This was an important moment of the Judaeo-Christian revelation.

It might help here to consider other possible scenarios. We assume nowadays that religious people should be moral. If they are not, we tend to think that there is something false about their religion. But are religion and morality necessarily connected? Can one be moral without belief in God? Can one believe in God without experiencing moral concern? In considering the issue we might keep in mind the two elements of morality which were mentioned in the first chapter—the distinction which we make between right and wrong behaviour (one's moral code) and the element of moral obligation (the sense we have that one *ought* to do what is right and avoid what is wrong).

The traditions of philosophy believe in the main that there is a morality that is independent of God. They believe that one can arrive at judgments about what is morally right and also that one can recognise moral obligation without recourse to a deity. If some sense can be given to the moral enterprise without religion we need to do some thinking about notions that would see morality originating in the commandments of God. We need to work out a position about the Ten Commandments and in particular to ask ourselves whether we understand them to have been directly given or commanded by God.

They were not given in the literal manner of the Bible story. It is much nearer the truth to think of Judaism assuming and accepting into itself the great natural experience of morality than to think of Judaism receiving moral commands directly from God. What the Jews came to realise was that as people of God they were to attend to this fundamental strand of human experience. If they were to be God's people they were to be moral people: they were to take seriously the horizontal dimension of their lives, their living with one another. Nothing could contribute more powerfully to that insight, nothing could give it greater weight and significance in Jewish minds that to attach morality to Moses, the great prophet, and to regard it as given to him by God as his law for his people. The insight about the significance of morality was important. But we need to distinguish between the reality of the insight and the particularly colourful and impressive way in which it was communicated.

In Judaism, then, there is obviously a close link between the notion of the deity and the experience of morality. (It would, of course, be interesting to ask what kind of interplay there was between the two elements in the developing Jewish consciousness. Presumably, developing insights about morality would in time be predicated of the deity. On the other hand, belief in a deity who had moral attributes would lead very naturally to a realisation that the people should also exhibit such moral attributes.) I have mentioned different scenarios. The question that arises for us here requires a brief look at religious experience and its institutionalisation. We need to broaden our vision to ask the more general question about the different elements which are found in religions and the ways in which they are combined or related.

RELIGION AND MORALITY: A STRUGGLE

There is great difficulty in arriving at satisfactory definitions of what we mean by religious experience or of the phenomenon which we refer to as religion. The best we can say is that there are certain family resemblances between experiences which people refer to as religious and between religions. We can roughly define a religion as a system of beliefs and practices by means of which a group struggles with the ultimate problems of life—Wach, for example, says that the fundamental themes in any statement of faith are the nature of the ultimate reality, the nature of the cosmos and the world, the nature of the human person.[1] There is much debate on the extent to which one can find common elements in religions. But it seems that a religion will try to cope with the problems that specify its area not only conceptually but emotionally and practically also. So it is likely that a religion will have some kind of faith (stories, myths), that it will propose some kind of attitude or response to the ultimate reality, and that this will include both cult and some directives for the practical issues of daily life (action-guides—moral or ethical teaching).

It is this last element which interests us here. Among religions which do have such an element the significance of it differs: indeed authors have tried to classify religions according to the prominence given to the ethical element. It could well be that, instead of the ethical, the ritual, for example, would pre-dominate: one can even point to instances where the role of a particular element has changed from one stage of a religion's history to another. It is clear that the ethical element is pro-minent in Christianity (so much so that for some it is nothing but ethics). But it is worth reflecting on the fact—it ought not to be taken for granted. Judaeo-Christianity has seen the rise and fall of different elements. Gnostic influences which would make knowledge supreme had their day and are never far from us. Dependence on ritual has been a constant temptation. The dilemma between engagement in the world and flight from it into contemplation has not been resolved easily. Ethical striving, the seeking of moral perfection, has been more or less prominent at different times.

It is especially instructive to note the bitter battle that was fought between the ritual and ethical elements in Old Testament times—if only because we have echoes of it in our own day. While we can trace back to Moses an insistence on the importance of morality, it was the failure of his people to align their lives with his insight that produced the great ethical outcry of the eighth century prophets—something that in itself was to colour the Moses story. The message of the prophets was that God is not honoured and will not be found by those who put their trust in ritual but who are unjust and unmindful of the widow and the orphan.

> I hate, I despise your feasts,
> and I take no delight in your solemn assemblies.
> Even though you offer me your burnt offerings and
> cereal offerings,
> I will not accept them,
> and the peace offerings of your fatted beasts
> I will not look upon.

Take away from me the noise of your songs;
to the melody of your harps I will not listen.
But let justice roll down like waters,
and righteousness like an ever-flowing stream.
(Amos 5:21-24)

'With what shall I come before the Lord,
and bow myself before God on high?
Shall I come before him with burnt offerings,
with calves a year old?
Will the Lord be pleased with thousands of rams,
with ten thousands of rivers of oil?...'
He has showed you ... what is good;
and what does the Lord require of you
but to do justice, and to love kindness,
and to walk humbly with your God? (Mic. 6:6-8)

'What to me is the multitude of your sacrifices?'
says the Lord;
'I have had enough of burnt offerings of rams
and the fat of fed beasts;
I do not delight in the blood of bulls,
or of lambs, or of he-goats....
Bring no more vain offerings;
incense is an abomination to me. ...
even though you make many prayers,
I will not listen....
cease to do evil, learn to do good;
seek justice, correct oppression;
defend the fatherless, plead for the widow.' (Is. 1:11ff)

The tension is, of course, a constant point of discussion
among Christians. We hear the question asked: who is the true
Christian, the one who goes to church or the one who cares for
his/her fellow human beings? What is to be made of the oft-
used expression 'a practising Catholic'; how valid is the perception that a practising Catholic is one who attends church; is
it a peculiarly Irish perception? We hear discussion about the
relation of life and liturgy, of prayer and politics. The emphasis
in recent times has been on the idea that faith is performative.
We have been told that the mark of the true Church is the

orthopraxis of justice rather than the orthodoxy of belief. We have seen the emergence of theologies of development and liberation: it is interesting that there is very explicit appeal in these theologies to the prophetic literature just mentioned and to Old Testament symbols of liberation and promise. We have been challenged by the idea that it is only those who are engaged in the political struggle for justice who can begin to understand what the Judaeo-Christian message is about.

The same tension appears in the New Testament. If you come to offer your gift at the altar but are at odds with your brother, leave your gift at the altar and go first and be reconciled with your brother. If you ask what is the greatest commandment, the answer is that it is to love God and your neighbour. If you ask who will possess the kingdom, it will not be those who put their faith in ritual practices or trust in their descent from Abraham but those who give to the hungry and the thirsty, who visit the sick and imprisoned. Religion that is pure and undefiled before God and the Father is this: to visit the widows and orphans in their affliction and to keep oneself unstained from the world (Jas. 1:27).

New Testament religion is highly moral. New Testament morality is religious: it is single-mindedly thought of in relation to God. God requires us to be moral: one should be moral because God is moral; in one's moral life one should be like God. We are to be perfect as our heavenly Father is perfect, be compassionate as he is in Christ, forgive as he has forgiven, love our enemies and pray for our persecutors. Only thus can we be children of our Father. Moral life is to be imitation, response, gratitude. It is discipleship of Christ and in large part moral discipleship. His life was one of moral concern and he is the norm. We are to learn from him, wash one another's feet, love one another as he has done, let our bearing towards one another arise out of our life in him. (Mt. 5; Jn. 13; Phil. 2:5)

Acts portrays a life of discipleship in which there is the closest possible connection between faith, liturgy and moral life (Acts 2:44 ff.). Just as in St John it is impossible to disentangle faith in Christ and love of the brethren (1 Jn. 1:6-7). One who fails in either way does not know God, does not know who God is or the kind of God in whom Christians believe. He/she cannot be in Christ and the Spirit. Indeed the very activity of God in us through Christ and his Spirit issues in

30

morality. God is love and his love is poured forth in our hearts by the Spirit that we may love: so the fruits of the Spirit are charity, peace, patience, kindness, gentleness, self-control (Rom. 8 and 5:5; Gal. 5:22). There is a mystical link between love of God and neighbour so that we cannot always discern when the New Testament speaks of one and when it speaks of the other.

What emerges from all this is that the Judaeo-Christian tradition has a strong moral strand and has situated morality very decisively in relation to God. It is an important part of the revelation that faith in God, following of Christ, membership of his people, involves a moral way. This is what people mean when they refer to Christian morality as covenant morality, invitation-response morality, discipleship. Note however that our concern so far has not been with what is right and wrong, with the actual material content of morality, with what the Bible says about what we ought to do—but rather with a range of issues that *situate* morality for the Christian, that give him/her a general attitude to or outlook on morality. Let us call this the context of Christian morality, as distinct from its (material) content. What we are dealing with is the manner in which the two areas of morality and religion become intertwined for the Christian. It is what some have referred to as the theological frontier of morality, the place at which morality becomes more than morality for Christians because of the many subtle ways in which their religious belief affects it.

CONTEXT: THE LAW OF GOD

Let us reflect a little on this religious *context* of morality within the Judaeo-Christian tradition. What the tradition most wanted to say was that God, who is creator and sustainer of life, in some way requires morality from us. While Christians can maintain a relative autonomy for morality they cannot regard it—any more than anything else in life—as absolutely autonomous. They cannot say what they want to say about the world and all its immanent activity and institutions without referring it to God. They cannot see morality as solely morality. They must somehow express their belief that it is God's world, that the institution of morality is consonant with God and his purposes, that, so to speak, it is part of what God willed human beings to discover about themselves. In some

31

way they must say that God is in this discovery, that we can only be who and what He wants us to be if we align our lives with this moral strand of our experience. This is something that is difficult to express. It is a species of God-talk. All God-talk is the use of our human language and experience to suggest something that is not entirely within the range of our experience: we can know what we experience but we cannot fully know who or what God is. So we are stuck with using terms from some other area of life to express what we want to say about God. The attempt to express this relationship between an autonomous morality and a Creator-God has been referred to as a 'baffling semantic task'.[2]

The manner of expressing it that suggested itself to the Jews was to say that the moral code was a treaty between a ruler and his people. It was the *law* of God. And as we saw, the obvious way to represent this was to portray God as *giving* his code of conduct to his people and enjoining its observance. This way of expressing one's understanding was accentuated in a medieval world that was very conscious of the relations of lord and servant, very much in tune with the notion of a lord who gives orders and organises the life of his underlings. The medievals thought of the universe as ordered by God, each part with its own plan. Plants have their law, animals have theirs, humans have theirs—the law of humans is their innate moral thrust. All was what the medieval called the eternal law, the great blue-print of the master craftsman designed and imposed by him on the universe. The later text books were so locked into the culture of law that they went to great trouble to prove that the eternal law was a true law, fulfilling all the conditions of law—they said that God as a lawgiver has promulgated his (moral) laws and has imposed a sanction on those who disobey.

The Hebrew story of the giving of the Decalogue, God's law, the medieval language of 'law of God' and in particular the text book insistence on law while they have a certain validity are fraught with problems. There is a danger of thinking of morality as a code of conduct coming from outside us, made by someone in authority and enjoined on us. That is how we usually think of a law. Such a notion applied to morality is clearly misleading: it runs counter to what we said in the previous chapter. God does not make morality, nor is it from God that the force or claim or obligation of morality comes.

32

Honesty is good in itself but it can be—and may need to be—*called* the law or will of God. Cruelty is wrong in itself but it can be said to be contrary to the will of God. God makes us but it is we who discover the moral dimension within ourselves and, so to speak, impose morality on ourselves. So too was it with Moses and the Jews. They had from within themselves some sense of the moral demand. They did not need to have it revealed by God. So whatever 'law of God' language might mean, it does not mean that morality or its binding force derive from God.

There are more nuanced understandings of law. For the great scholastics it signified essentially guidance towards an end. 'Law' is, after all, an analogical term and we use it to describe the law of the seasons as well as the law of nature or physical laws. I could refer to morality as the law of my being, as a thrust in me, a tendency to move or grow in a particular direction—a thrust, for example, to act in a way that brings about my good or flourishing or development. And I can of course say that in this sense morality is the law or will of God my Creator. But there is all the difference in the world between thinking of human beings listening to a thrust in them to behave in a particular way and finding it appropriate to refer to this *also* as the will or law of God, and thinking of morality as the law of God because it is a set of ordinances issued by him. It was in the former sense that the great scholastics could refer to morality as law and in this attenuated sense as the law of God. We can still do so today provided we know what we are doing.

It is possible to speak of morality, of duty, of moral claim without referring to God. But it is not possible for a believer to express adequately his/her total view of things without making some attempt to contextualise all things, morality included, in God. To refer to morality then as the law or will of God, or in some such terms, is a much more comprehensive way of understanding it, and for him/her a necessary description of his/her world. But the language of 'law' or 'will' with which we are familiar in our daily lives and experiences cannot be transferred without great logical caution to God and morality. We do not do justice to the notion of morality unless we somehow preclude the deduction that God is a man with a 'will' who issues commands like a ruler or sergeant-major and who arranges for punishment for those who do not obey.

It may be that we need to reverse our thinking about the expressions 'law' or 'will' of God. When people refer to something as being against the law or will of God they seem to mean that it is against some decree that God made at some time in the past or some direction that he now wishes to give. But this is a misapprehension. Whatever is right is the will of God, whatever is wrong is contrary to the will of God. If we have discovered what is morally right we have *then* discovered the will of God—not vice versa—and it is our only way of discovering it. Of course, in many situations in life we may have great difficulty in discovering what is morally right and therefore what is the will of God. That is a problem with which we have to live. God does not make everything clear to us. There is no good reason to expect that the will of God will be easily accessible to us, because there is no good reason to expect that we can be absolved from the difficult search for what is the morally right judgment. So an authority cannot easily assert that a decree or rule is the will of God: the will of God has to be sought. What is required of us is an honest search for the best course of action in the circumstances: even then all we can have is a presumption. Perhaps we have been too facile about that in the past. We are not just being difficult or disloyal then if we question one who declares that something is the will of God—individual, society, Church.

However there is a major issue which might suggest itself here and which we will take up later. It is this: if our tradition has been convinced that a particular position is the morally right one and therefore the will of God, what authority does that have for us now? It is the question of the authority of the Bible and of Church declarations. However the Ten Commandments, for example, were arrived at—in whatever manner they were 'received'—they are now part of the Bible. What is the significance of that? Does the fact that they are in the Bible and that they have been accepted by the apostolic Church as the revelation of God not indicate the will of God for us? That is a question that will have to wait.

CONTEXT: SUPPORT AND MOTIVATION FOR MORAL LIFE

The Christian does not merely want to say that God is Creator, source, ruler of all things, and that therefore we must in some sense refer to morality as his law or will. The relations between accepting the moral dimension and believing in the Christian God are many-faceted. There are all sorts of relationships. (As we hinted already, the particular perspective in which a religious person will see morality will in some fashion depend on his/her understanding of the deity.) In a religion in which a deity is immoral or capricious morality will not be important. In some religions God may be otiose or indifferent to the world, or his/her creation may be devoid of moral purpose. Or God may be evil or immoral or there may be in him/her a struggle of good and evil. But over the ages Christians have come to a view of the deity—a fusion of the God of Abraham, Isaac and Jacob with the God of the Greek philosophers—who is rational, intelligent, purposeful, morally perfect, loving. This affects the Christian view of morality profoundly. There is a harmony between belief in an intelligent God and the pursuance of rational (moral) activity, between belief in a loving God and the humanising activity of morality, between the struggle to lead a virtuous life and assimilation to the deity. There is massive support in the Christian stories for the whole moral effort. Christians have a faith in the possibility of true response to others. They have a trust in the power of God in the midst of difficulties. They have a viewpoint on the final significance of the moral enterprise. They have a resurrection-hope in the future even in the face of apparent failure. They have a confidence in the forgiveness of the Ultimate Reality however intractable our wills and hearts. Christianity provides a world-view or climate that is favourable to morality.

In addition, there is in Christianity what is more precisely a motivation for moral living. Right through the Old and New Testaments there is what has been called the indicative-imperative dialectic. God is good: we ought to be good. He is merciful, faithful, long-suffering: we should imitate him. He is Father of the poor, the one who cares for the widow and orphan, the liberator of the oppressed, the one who forgives and blesses enemies: so should we be. Christ has forgiven his enemies, has emptied himself, has laid down his life for us: we should learn from that. We are his body, are risen with him, have new life in him: we should live as such. We have received the Spirit: we should walk in the Spirit and bring forth the fruits of the Spirit. There is no doubt but that this kind of motivation has been powerful in the lives of Christians through the ages and has enabled them to undertake lives of great moral devotion and sacrifice. Their faith has given them reasons for acting, objectives to aim at—God's rule, his kingdom, his plan. It has given them examples to move them—the story of what God has done for us in Christ. It has given them an understanding of themselves—God's elect, Christ's disciples, the community of the Spirit. All of this has given a tone and power to Christian morality—it all belongs to the Christian context of morality.

MORALITY AND SALVATION: MODELS

But even more crucial in shaping the Christian consciousness of morality has been something that is closely related to the notion of morality as law of God. That is the relation of morality and salvation. This has so dominated Christian, certainly Catholic, consciousness that many have thought salvation to be the main reason and justification for moral effort. There are religions which do not believe the soul to be immortal or to be dependent on God, or which have no notion of reward or punishment in the afterlife. But in Christianity there is the closest relation between morality, immortality and salvation. We were taught as children that those who are morally good go to heaven, to union with God—the morally bad go to hell. Certainly there is much in the Old and especially in the New Testament to warrant this view.

If the story of the giving of the Ten Commandments has dominated Christianity with regard to the source and understanding of morality, the other great story which has dominated it with regard to the final point or significance of morality has been Matthew25. 'When the Son of man comes in his glory, and all the angels with him, then he will sit on his glorious throne. Before him will be gathered all the nations, and he will separate them one from another. . . . Then the King will say to those at his right hand, "Come, O blessed of my Father, inherit the Kingdom prepared for you from the foundation of the world. . ."' This was taken up into the idea of the great general judgment which was seen as an accounting of one's whole moral life. At the theological level it was again the text book that copperfastened this idea. God gives the moral law, it declared: he commands us to observe it; by observing it we can merit heaven which will be given to us as a reward; if we refuse, God owes it to himself to impose on us the ultimate sanction of hell. And so through the centuries millions have been encouraged into or terrified into observing the moral way by the hope of heaven or the fear of hell. There is involved here not just a particular idea of morality but a particular idea of God.

It is strange how little attention has been paid in Catholic morality to this general question of the relation of moral life to salvation (beatific vision) and in particular how little we have reflected on how our tradition has shaped this area of our consciousness. Perhaps it is because we have so easily gone along with the traditional answers. The problem is not a new one. We find that Aristotle had a problem about the link between moral perfection and contemplation. One can see that this is also the problem which Christianity had to face—what is the relation between moral goodness and beatific vision. Is morality—living well with society—a precondition of beatitude (contemplation of God)? Is life a test to be passed? How do we hold the various elements—God, morality, salvation—together?

The model which won out was the law-merit-reward model, what Karl Rahner calls the forensic model, and about which he is unhappy.[3] This sees beatific vision as a reward that is granted for moral goodness, but a reward that is extrinsic to it and has no inherent connection with it. It is on the lines of 'If you are a good boy/girl I will buy you a bicycle for Christmas'. Is there any connection here between behaviour and reward except the arbitrary one of a promise made by someone who has power to deliver on that promise? One finds a somewhat more satisfactory model in Aquinas who views moral life as a preparation for vision, who says that only those who are morally good are apt or in a condition to receive beatific vision—so that it is not entirely extrinsic. Rahner himself suggests—and this is found in the best of Christian philosophy—that one who responds morally to the various situations of life is in truth responding to God although he/she may not actually think of or refer his/her life to God. You could say that when one seeks the true good it is really God whom one is seeking—God is the 'beyond', the horizon of one's choice. He is the Truth, the

Good. God cannot be grasped or attained directly: it is only by choosing the proximate good, i.e. by moral choice in respect of others, that one can make a choice about or determine one's attitude to him. In this way moral choice is seen to be much more than moral choice. In the end it is choice for or against God. One who in the totality of his/her life has established a pattern of moral goodness is in his/her basic attitude attuned to God, choosing God. So that the whole incalculable mystery of the human being is contained in moral choice. He/she is judging him/herself, has decided whether to respond to God's offer of friendship and union or not. This is the freedom which God has given to us.[4]

I have been referring to models. I mean the manner in which we hold together these very fundamental issues in our thinking (and emotional life)—God, morality, salvation. We all need to ask ourselves what model we are operating out of. It affects very much not only our idea of morality but our idea of God. John Robinson, then Bishop of Woolwich, said in *Honest to God* that one cannot change one's notion of God without changing one's notion of morality. The contrary is also true. It is arguable that the notion of God most familiar to Christians generally is one that is greatly coloured by considerations of morality and salvation. Indeed it is arguable that if young people today reject God it is this ethical God with his judgment and everlasting punishments in hell that they are rejecting. The question that must be asked is whether this is the true God. Is it a conception of God that has emerged out of specific cultural forms which were used to accommodate the thorny question of the relation of morality to God?

Some branches of Christianity adopt a quite different approach. Protestantism in general does not attach salvation to moral living in the same way. It breaks the merit-reward mould—which appears to suggest that we gain or possess or can in some sense claim God in return for moral goodness. The Protestant understanding puts God and his gracious forgiveness first: someone summed it up by saying that we accept ourselves as having being accepted in spite of being unacceptable. There should be moral life, it insists, but it is in response to, in gratitude for justification freely given us by God in Christ rather than a means to it. The justified person does the works of love. But it is not works that win salvation.

This takes us into an area of Christian faith that has been the point of deep division among Christians. The pursuit of it would take us far afield. I make just three brief points here. The first is that I find among Christians generally a subtle desire to move away from the traditional model which I have outlined and to ease into something that approximates to the Protestant tradition. There is, I believe, among Christians a shift in their notion of God towards emphasis on his mercy and forgiveness. One rarely hears talk nowadays about merit and reward. One rarely hears the sermons of earlier days. There is a discernible softening of lines. This is saying something to the community and its theologians. How, I wonder, has it come about? Second, at the reflective theological level one finds among theologians a clear wish to rethink issues around morality and salvation. One finds it in the massive work that has been done on justification by Küng and Rahner. But one finds it also in more incidental pieces. Third, one cannot pass over in silence the immense scarring of the personality that has occurred because of the fearsome and terrifying sermons that arose out of the God-morality-salvation model as received in the Catholic Church. As I say, there is a perceptible shift. But any priest who has sat in the confessional will have had depressing experiences of the fear and anxiety with which at least many of our older people have approached God.

WHY BE MORAL?

Built into the general question of models which we have been discussing is the question: why be moral? The answer most commonly given in the past was that one should be moral because God commands it; or at best that one should be moral out of love of God—'if you love me keep my commandments'. One can see that this approach will not do. It is what led some philosophers to describe religious morality as infantile. It will not do because moral claims are not to be justified in the first place—whatever about being justified in the last place—in terms of God.[5] How then are they to be justified?

It is a very curious thing this business of moral claim, this 'I could not/you cannot' which we looked at in the previous chapter. Christian philosophers and theologians have argued about it and some—but only some—have thought that the

39

unconditional character of moral obligation requires a final grounding in God. But one cannot ignore the fact that moral philosophers generally believe that they can justify morality, can give an answer to the question 'Why be moral?', without an appeal to God. Some see it this way: that it is as native to us to recognise that certain kinds of action are not to be done as it is to recognise, for example, that the whole is greater than the part; it is a demand of our reason and we do as much violence to ourselves by denying one as the other; that is what carries the 'ought' for them. Others relate it more to the insight that persons are to be respected and that there is some dissonance in us if we do not do so. Others to some intuition about the rights of persons. Others to an insight that it only makes sense to do the action that brings about the most human good. Others to a sense of fairness or impartiality—that we should treat others as we would have them treat us—or to a conviction that anything else is illogical. Others to an understanding of what it means to be a true human being in society, to the art of being a flourishing person in a society that functions satisfactorily. Their perception is that one needs to acquire certain virtues if society and its members are to reach their purpose: it presupposes that we have a kind of nature that has a potential for perfection (which corresponds to our deepest desires): if we live a certain manner of life we reach that, if we do not we fail to reach it; any further notion of 'ought' that has the implication of obligation is seen by them as a relic of a time of universal faith when God was accepted as a moral authority.

Whether one can be given a convincing answer to the question 'Why be moral?' depends on whether any of these considerations have an appeal. 'Why' is a demand for convincing reasons. But the kind of reason which will convince depends on one's interests. There may not be much point in proposing the considerations of the last paragraph to one whose only active interests are the grosser pleasures of life—you would find it hard to answer the question 'Why be moral?' if you had to answer it for someone in those terms. Or if it had to be answered in terms of 'What is in it for me?'. There *is* something in it for us but it is at a deep level and whether or not it will convince depends on the character we have: we may not be open to such considerations; so it may be a vain enterprise to try to convince us.

It is considerations of this kind that are the stuff of morality. Being moral means awakening to and growing into such considerations. It is a matter of responsibility and maturity to know why one has moral positions and why one assents to living by them. The more personal, deliberate and interior this is the more human and valuable it is. Simply doing what one is told to do because one is told to do it is not a very advanced state of moral life. And indeed not one that should be encouraged by the style of moral teaching or education. It is instructive to ask ourselves questions of this kind. Try it: why do you think you should do X? You will probably answer by saying that doing X is right because it is doing Y—that paying taxes is good because it enables a better society to be created or brings about more human good. But why should you be concerned about that? It is when you push yourself back to that question that you find yourself struggling with moral theory.

Moralists may and do disagree about the foundation of their theories. But what there will be agreement about is that the fundamental reason for being moral is a reason from within the area of morality. The fundamental appeal of the moral teacher or reformer will be a moral one—do not kill or practise apartheid or exploit or plan nuclear war will be justified in terms of rationality or respect or fairness or benevolence or flourishing or rights. What this is saying is that the moral claim should not be short-circuited by immediately attaching it to God. The appeal is a human appeal—an appeal to what it means to be a human person. This is what we must try to listen to in ourselves and encourage in others. To think of morality or moral claim predominantly in terms of God at least runs the risk of devaluing it: it is possible for religion to do a disservice to morality.

What this means is that for religious people there are different reasons for being moral. There are moral reasons, i.e. reasons which arise out of the kind of consideration mentioned above. These are central to morality, all morality, including Christian morality. They are what morality is about. There are also religious reasons, e.g. because it is the will of God or to become like him, or as an act of love of God or to bring about his plan or purposes or kingdom. Both kinds of reasons are good; religion can help and encourage morality. But to be moral solely for (religious) reasons extrinsic to morality appears to lack true awareness of the human claim that is morality. The traditional *dictum* says that grace builds on nature: what is bad morality cannot be good Christianity. So St Thomas has the striking statement: 'He therefore who avoids evil not because it is evil but because of the command of God is not free, but he who avoids evil because it is evil is free'.[6] There is also the danger that if the only reason we have for being moral is a religious one we will be left morally marooned if religious commitment weakens.

Our conclusion must be something along the following lines. Morality is a phenomenon that is independent of religion. One can arrive at moral positions or codes without religion. One can give a sense to the notion of moral call or demand or obligation or law without it. But if one is a religious person and particularly if one is a Christian one's view of morality will be affected in various ways—one's view of the place which morality occupies in the total scheme of things and how it occupies that place. For many Christians morality is the place where they meet God and can make a practical response to him. It is the daily test and struggle of discipleship. The moral question for many has been transmuted into the questions: how am I to respond to God or express union with him; what does Christ want; what does following him in faith mean? The Christian then might well see God as the ultimate context, significance and end of moral living without compromising the notion of morality as an autonomous human experience.

MAKING MORAL DECISIONS:
THE BIBLE

THE issues raised in the last chapter are important for
Christian moral life. But for most people they are not the key
issues. The key issues are: (*a*) what is right and wrong?; (*b*) how
do I find out what is right and wrong?; (*c*) why do we say that
something is right or wrong? The substantive issue for most of
us is not why we are to behave morally or how we can be helped
by Christian faith to do so, but what we are to do or what we
may do. Is it alright to...? Is it wrong to...? Or to put it in its
notorious form, How far may I go...? I refer to this as the
content of morality—to be contrasted with its general context
(which we have considered already).

The three questions here are different questions. A possible
response might take in all three. (*a*) Divorce is wrong; (*b*) I
know it is wrong because the Church tells me (or God tells me
or tells the Church through his revelation which is found in the
Bible); (*c*) it is wrong because it is a hurt or offence to the
human being to whom I have promised life-long commitment
(or because it is a serious blow to society which needs a
permanent institution of marriage or because it breaches the
likeness to Christ and his Church which marriage is to mirror
forth). I just offer these as samples of answers.

In this chapter I concentrate on the question: how do we
find out what is right or wrong? I want to deal in particular
with the idea that God tells us what is right/wrong and that we
find what he has to say about that in the Bible. Christians frequently refer to the Bible in moral matters. How often have
you heard 'It says in the Bible' or 'it is in the Ten Commandments': remember the manner in which biblical texts
were cited at the time of the 1986 divorce referendum in
Ireland. The Bible is appealed to as in some sense an

authoritative source of information—because the plan or will or purposes of God are thought to be contained there.

Why should we need God to tell us about morality? Well, for some people there may still be hanging around the idea that God makes rules or regulations for our lives: we saw that there is a lot of vagueness about the notion of morality as the *law* of God and about the Ten *Commandments.* Certainly we depend on God for our faith. It is because he has made himself known to the Jewish people particularly through its prophets and to the New Testament community in Jesus Christ that we know what kind of God he is—good, loving, merciful, close to us, concerned about our world, a Trinity—and that we know about the incarnation, salvation, our future with God etc. We say that he has revealed this. Some naturally consider that we depend on him equally to tell us what our lives are to be like, how we are to live, what is good or bad, pleasing to him or displeasing. They consider therefore that revelation extends not only to who God is and what are his plans for us but also to how we are to live.

It is important to note that to say that God tells us what is right and wrong is not the same as saying the God makes right and wrong. I have been stressing that God does not make morality as a ruler makes laws but rather that acts (as well as intentions, attitudes, thoughts etc.) are right or wrong in themselves—cruelty is wrong because it is cruelty. In (c) above we did not say that divorce is wrong because God said so or made it a rule. However, one might well say that things are right/wrong in themselves but also say that we are not very good at working out the details of this. For example, parents and teachers may well have the good of a child at heart but may be at a loss to know what is best for the child and may seek advice from someone else.

On the matter of information about moral living one could roughly divide the Christian tradition in two. There are those who think that we need God to tell us how to live. They may hold this for two reasons: (i) because we human beings are not very good at figuring out right and wrong on our own; (ii) because as disciples of Jesus Christ we know that human beings have been received into a special relationship with God about the implications of which only God can enlighten us. On the other hand there are those who believe not only that morality is a human phenomenon but also that we are pretty good at working out on our own how to live—without the special revelation which God is said to have made to Jews and Christians. They say that human beings generally know something about what is an appropriate form of living and together can work out most of the details. (It is recognised that some are better than others at it—that some, as we said in the first chapter, are stupid, perverse, depraved or morally blind.)'That is very roughly what is meant by the theory of natural law.

So we have two main lines. However, there is an intermediate position. Some hold that although we can work out the demands of moral living pretty well on our own, God has in fact also revealed to his people the demands of such living, and further, that while we can theoretically understand it without this special revelation it is difficult for us to do so 'easily, with certitude and without admixture of error'. This was the position of Vatican I and it is the current orthodoxy of the Catholic Church. Therefore it is quite common for official Catholic statements to refer both to rational argument and to revelation in support of its positions. Look up any recent document on moral matters either from a Roman Congregation or from local hierarchies and you will find this: e.g. the 1975 document on sexual ethics *(Persona Humana)*, the 1974 teaching on abortion, the 1986 letter on the pastoral care of homosexuals, the teaching on indissolubility *(Familiaris Consortio*, 1981). Often the document indicates specific biblical passages or texts as proof of its position. But sometimes it makes a more generalised reference to the foundation of its position in revelation. For example *Humanae Vitae* claims to base its teaching on 'natural law illumined by revelation' and *Laborem Exercens* (the letter of Pope John Paul II on work) says that the Church's social teaching finds its source in Scripture. So that when the Church teaches it seems to depend on two sources for its knowledge of what is right—reason and revelation.

The net result of this double appeal to reason and revelation is that in many instances the final recourse is to the Bible even for fundamental moral rules. Problems naturally arise because intelligent and skilled people — perhaps some who have worked extensively in philosophical ethics or who have experience in a particular area, e.g. marriage—for one reason or another disagree with the Church's position. Recourse to biblical texts then or a generalised reference to revelation looks like a retreat into some kind of ghetto or esoteric morality. The argument is no longer a matter of reason against reason, of rational discussion. The weapons have changed, the Church is using the authority of revelation (of which it claims to be the only competent interpreter) or of Scripture to found its position, even though it is still claimed as a position that is theoretically intelligible to all. It is saying to the philosopher or to the person in the street that he/she is unable to canvass the capacities of reason, that—whatever the cause of his/her problem—he/she is blind to the true solution on this point. This is not an attitude that is likely to be greeted warmly by the non-religious or by those outside of Catholicism. But there are many within Catholicism who have problems with it also. In particular they ask if it is possible to look to the Bible for moral guidance in this way. This chapter will be partly about this controversy which surrounds the Church's use of the Bible in arriving at the well-known moral rules which it proposes to us. I shall come back to that. But first I want to develop a little the notion of the content of morality.

We have mentioned something of the Church's official teaching. But what the Church says in official teaching is very limited: all it gives—just as all the Ten Commandments give—is a few basic rules for a few select areas of life. One could not regard the Ten Commandments or the teaching of the Church as an adequate map for living. The richness and variety of our lives cannot be caught only in a few rules. Our lives are not only about the Ten Commandments but about the quirks and twists of our individual situations and the potentialities and possibilities which only we have. They are unique, personal and varied. Nobody can give any of us a total blueprint for our lives. We have to take on ourselves the burden of our decisions.

In the end we have to approach our lives on our own. For example: How do you fairly deal with a child who is causing chaos in the family or the classroom? What political programmes should you support? Are you entitled not to declare some of your earnings? Should you separate from a husband who beats you and terrifies your children? What are your obligations towards the Third World? What action should you take about U.S. involvement in Nicaragua? Should you protest about the visit of a dictator to this country? Your mother/father who lives with you upsets your spouse and children—should you put him/her in a home? You have a handicapped child in the family or the classroom—what proportion of time should you give him/her relative to the other children? How are you to respond to your husband's/wife's infidelity? What are your obligations to someone with whom you have established a deep relationship? Should you try to influence your children's life choices? What response should you make to a life-style which you think harmful to them? Should you leave your aged parents in order to work in the Third World or pursue your career abroad? To what extent should you go along with the agitation of your pressure group for a larger share of the national cake? Are you justified in accepting the fees which your profession has managed to demand for its services? About such matters neither the Ten Commandments nor the official teaching of the Church will be of much help. You could, of course, ask your local priest but that is a different matter: that is not the teaching of the church; you are only asking the opinion of someone like yourself who may be no wiser than you are.

A SPECIFIC CHRISTIAN MORALITY?
DOES ONE NEED THE BIBLE?

About such matters one cannot easily elaborate moral rules. And yet they are the content of our lives and of our morality, along with a host of other issues, opportunities and temptations—opportunities to take more than our fair share of the burden, to forget ourselves for the sake of others; temptations to take advantage, to cheat and hoard, to insist on our share at all costs, to be enclosed in our own ambitions, to be seduced by riches. How are we to make our decisions? What light can we get—and from where? Should we look to the Bible? I could put the question this way: how am I as a Christian, as a follower of Christ to respond to these life situations? To put the question in this form is to raise an interesting angle, i.e. whether the words 'as a Christian', 'as a follower of Christ' have any significance in the question: that has become a matter of serious debate.

Some Catholic theologians think that they do not—that

what is required of a Christian in his/her moral life is the same as what is required of any human being. That means also for them that what is required of a Christian can be discovered by any right-thinking person: they do not see the Christian faith or story either as requiring anything special in moral living or as offering any special insight. This affects their attitude to the Bible. They see no need for a revelation of morality. Indeed they assert that there is nothing in the moral teaching of the Bible that is not available outside it. And they claim that even if one were to concede that there is a moral revelation one would find the problem of using the Bible so overwhelming as to make it impracticable. They acknowledge that one may legitimately turn to the Bible for encouragement and motivation in moral life but disallow appeal to it for any substantive guidance.

There are others, as we have seen, who are unhappy with this. They believe that we need guidance and that God intends to instruct us through the Bible. They see it as an indispensable source of information about moral life. There has been a very strong movement among Catholic authors since the fifties in favour of a Bible-centred morality. They were reacting against what had been presented up to the time as moral theology, mere natural law morality, which they found minimalist and uninspiring. They regarded it as not entirely worthy of Christian life. The central point for them was that Christian life must be nourished by the Scriptures and that moral theology must be biblical through and through, must grow out of the great biblical themes. This point of view received considerable endorsement in the decrees of Vatican II which urged that moral theology be 'more thoroughly nourished by Scripture teaching' which it referred to as 'the soul of all theology'. That was an attractive suggestion but it was soon to be described as 'naive biblicism' because it was found that there are great difficulties in the use of the Bible in moral matters.

To rule out appeal to the Bible, as some do, appears to go contrary to the practice of the Christian community. Preachers, theologians, Church documents and Christians generally seek guidance from the Bible (although theologians often say that we are more at sea in our appeal to the Bible in moral matters than in other areas of Christian life). Moral guidance can be given in ways that are more general or more precise. Examples of the first kind are: respect life; be perfect as

48

your heavenly Father is perfect; love one another as Christ has loved us; seek justice; be gracious and kind. These propose values, aims and ideals to us but they do not give us exact direction on what to do. Examples of the second kind are: do not commit adultery; do not divorce your wife and marry another. These are rules and they give exact direction. The questions for us are: what kind of direction can we expect to get from the Bible; in what way is it to bear on our judgments; how are we to use it? Can we expect to find precise rules there to direct us or only something more general? Those who believe that the Bible should bear authoritatively on moral discernment form a wide spectrum of opinion. They range from those who see it as a source of authoritative and permanently valid rules (e.g. that divorce, pre-marital sex and homosexual acts are always wrong), to those who see it as a revealed reality (rather than a revealed morality) that influences moral judgments. By that I mean that they see it as the source of a faith which will shape us and in an oblique way affect the judgments we make today rather than as a source of authoritative moral information. In between are those who see it as a source of general values, aims and ideals—much less stringent than rules—or who find in it moral paradigms or a kernel of permanent validity which might be differently lived from age to age.

At the back of some of these views are differing understandings of just how God has revealed himself and his purposes to us, i.e. about the manner of revelation. If what God wants to say to us is found in the Bible, just how did he 'say' it in the first place to the inspired writer? An earlier view of revelation saw it as a set of truths which God communicated by special insight to a particular prophet or sacred writer and which were later committed to writing in the Bible. Revelation-talk nowadays is not about truths passively received by an individual and passed on to the community for its acceptance on the authority of God, but about the fact that God reveals himself in human history, that within human communities and their traditions he enables his spiritual creatures to enter into an awareness of him. It is through the faith of the community and of particular people within it that revelation occurs. This is, however, a faith that is subject to the limitations of its time. The Bible is indeed our privileged access to

God. But what we have there are not timeless truth-propositions passively accepted but a faith and a revelation that bear the mark of the questions, the presuppositions, the world-view and the language of those who were actively involved in receiving it. One's understanding of this process of revelation will affect the manner in which one will understand the authority of the biblical text.

PROBLEMS ABOUT DEPENDENCE ON THE BIBLE

It has to be acknowledged that there are problems about holding that the Bible gives us permanently valid universal rules, even though a number of Churches make direct appeal to them.[1] Immediately there are problems about the meaning and applicability of texts—the meaning of the exceptive clause 'except on the ground of unchastity' in Matthew 5:32 and of the texts on homosexuality, masturbation and pre-marital sex used in *Persona Humana*. There is also question about whether one can speak of *the* ethical teaching of the Bible—we have two traditions on indissolubility, for example, one from Matthew and the other from First Corinthians. There is a general problem about imposing philosophical categories on a literature that did not envisage them, in particular about whether we can be confident that the imperatives of the Bible are to be interpreted as exceptionless moral rules—as distinct from *prima facie* principles, presumptions, or ideals. Take 1 Cor 7. It contains thirty six imperatives and uses a great variety of prescriptive words. To what extent are they to be understood as rules—or which of them and why?

One is aware too that some of the sacred writers were dependent on the philosophical ethics of the day (cf. the lists of vices and virtues—taken from pagan philosophy—in Colossians 3:18 and 4:1; Ephesians 5:22 and 6:9; 1 Corinthians 6:9-11; Galatians 5:16-25). The question is the significance to be given to the incorporation of such an ethic into the sacred texts: is there some Christian principle of choice at work that raises this pagan list to a new level and gives it precedence over anything that a later philosophy or theology, with perhaps a greater insight into human nature and psychology, could offer?—homosexuality is an obvious case in point. An even more serious matter is the very understandable limitation of the authors by their own cultural horizon—a number of official Roman documents, including the recent letter on the pastoral care of homosexuals, actually acknowledge this problem but then dismiss it. The well known instances are those concerning slaves and women—even when due allowance is made for the writer's attempt to introduce a new Christian nuance into the relationship ('wives, be subject to your husbands, as is fitting *in the Lord*'). An approach to the Bible that does not build in reservations about its cultural horizon is naive. An approach that does so opens every biblical imperative to re-examination. The problem then becomes one of finding a criterion for accepting some injunctions and rejecting others. How do we know or why do we say that we are not to be bound by what the Bible says about slavery or about the subjection of women to men or about the silence of women in Church? Some see this as a decisive objection to all biblical ethics and assert that we are left with no alternative but to subject everything to unaided philosophical judgment or, if you like, to common sense.

In spite of these reservations it has been firmly maintained by influential theologians that we have in the Bible permanently valid moral propositions which bind us today as God's will because, they say, there is an unbreakable link between them and the unchanging faith of the community. This, they contend, lifts them out of their cultural limitations and gives them lasting authority as rules. To say that there is in the Bible a linking of faith considerations and ethical considerations is true and important. Indeed much of the splendid energy of the biblical theologians of the forties and fifties went into delineating this—what some called the indicative-imperative structure of biblical ethics. To adduce a faith consideration in favour of a particular piece of behaviour is by implication to favour that behaviour. But that does not mean that the faith consideration is a justification or is put forward as a justification for the ethical position. The sacred writers often canvassed faith themes (new being/life in Christ/gift of the Spirit/membership of the Body) to encourage the believer to lead a moral life, to follow his/her conscience—and one does not want to play down the importance for today of that kind of exhortatory (parenetic) material. But the issue is whether a strict moral position is derived from a faith theme, whether there

51

are in the Bible moral rules that can be seen to be a necessary demand of a truth of faith—and therefore valid for all time.

The appeal to the Bible as a source of immutable moral *rules* is a rather limited one in the Church even if it has been at the heart of recent controversies. The Christian community uses the Bible in a much wider and more interesting variety of ways than this. To admit to difficulty with the Bible as a source of authoritative rules is not to reject its authority in morals—only to reject a particular kind of authority. The notion of the link of faith and ethics is still a useful key but a less rigid understanding of it allows one to take account of the constraints of culture, theology and perspective on the writers. It fits better with an appreciation that revelation is not only a message of divine provenance but a human product, that it could not come to us in timelessly valid categories and that even a so-called permanent moral kernel cannot be easily shelled out of its necessary cultural form.

A REVEALED REALITY:
FAITH AND THE 'I' WHO JUDGES

The suggestion that we think of the Bible as a source of a revealed reality rather than of a revealed morality is helpful, but I think we need to go even further and try to probe how the faith-understanding of the apostolic community (the revealed reality) pointed in particular ethical directions. One sees the link not so much between faith and immutable rules as between faith and more general values (goods), aims, dispositions, perspectives, intentions—which seem to be a constant of faith but which will be allowed to express themselves differently from one age to another. Moral discernment will not then be a matter of passively accepting revealed propositions but will be a more dynamic activity.

What I wish to point to is that we depend on the Bible for the great formative stories that tell us who we are and what the world and the human community are about, that these stories have a bearing on moral judgment, and that we find clues to that judgement in the ethical material of the Bible—I mean our stories about the Creator-Father of Our Lord Jesus Christ, about exodus and covenant, about incarnation, kingdom, forgiveness, death-resurrection, about Christ in us our hope of

52

glory. We might think of the effect that such stories have on the subject of moral discernment, on the 'I' who judges: it is the Christian subject's experience of life in Christ that should form the perspective of his/her ethics. Judgments are not made in a vacuum. They are made by people who see the world in a particular way because they are particular sorts of people. One's evaluative description of the field of action and the responsibility which is experienced in a situation depend on the sort of person one is. That in turn depends on the stories and symbols that shape one's consciousness and imagination. Religious faith might be seen as forming or having the potential to form a particular kind of character and therefore to suggest values and to evoke certain kinds of awareness and sensibility which affect moral judgment. One might see the Christian community as having its own character, formed by stories of what God has done for us in Christ.

That community lives in a tradition and the Bible is the classic of that tradition. To make a sharp distinction, as some have done, between its religious and its moral message is to fail to appreciate the coherence and consistency of its life. 'And they devoted themselves to the apostles' teaching and fellowship, to the breaking of bread and the prayers.... And all who believed were together and had all things in common; and they sold their possessions and goods and distributed them to all, as any had need.' (Acts 2; 42ff). This vignette of Acts finds support in the intermingling of belief and life in John: if we fail to love the brethren we are in the dark just as much as if we fail to recognise the Word; one who so fails does not know who God is. (1 Jn.) What we have in the Bible is an attempt of the apostolic community to put its faith into practice. 'What are we to *do*?' was its question to Jesus, Peter and Paul: it is the same question as we have today and it would be odd if it had nothing to tell us today—if the religious message (on which we so clearly depend) could be so divorced from living that the moral elements could be excised as an irrelevance. The Bible gives us an impression—impressions—of the apostolic community's experience of transcendence, of the imagination of those who experienced the inbreak of the kingdom in Jesus. It has much to say about action—about living, loving and dying, about world, flesh and devil, about wholeness and flourishing, about success and failure, about weakness and sin. In and through all of it one is confronted with an integrated ethico-mystical core which embodies the rooted experience of the apostolic community. What is important is that we be able to enter into this world of religious and moral meaning, that we allow the biblical text to challenge and change us, to open up for us the new and wider world of meaning that arises out of the experience of the divine irruption into history in Jesus Christ.

To say this is to speak very generally. But one cannot do much better. The ethical material of the Bible is rich, diverse and chaotic. It comes at several levels. Its language is not that of a scientific treatise but of literature—imaginative, colourful, taking its licence. Its mode is indicative, imperative, parabolic, mystical. It is more story than history, more wisdom than law. It says what it has to say in a bewildering profusion of forms and genres—in narrative, parable, 'saying', paradox, apocalypse. Its logic is elusive. (How does one move from symbols of new life, kingdom, vine-branches, body-members to conclusions about living? And yet it emerges that the writers did perceive a relationship between life in Christ and living in the world.) Its authority is difficult to pin down. (How does one find parable or paradox normative? 'He who finds his life will lose it, and he who loses his life for my sake will find it' [Mt. 10:39]. Only by entering into the logic of parable or paradox and letting them become the focal point of discernment.)

NOT READY-MADE JUDGMENTS

The use of the Bible is far from being the acceptance of ready-made judgments—moral rules—that one can immediately apply to current situations but is rather a dialogue between faith today and the complex, many-faceted faith of the apostolic community. It requires that we try to enter into the interplay of ethos and ethic which one can somehow chart in that community, to discover its bridge between believing and being-doing. It is not only what the texts say to us that is important. It is why the writers say what they say. It is their understanding of themselves and the elusive way in which they see the implications of that for living. I think we agree today that our preconscious sense of ourselves affects our questions, our perceptions and our aspirations, so we find ourselves trying to explore also the upper reaches of a biblical writer's world-view. You could say that we are looking for what made him tick. Not all can be uncritically accepted: the favoured perspective of our own faith will filter out, for example, a writer's expectation of an imminent return of the Lord and the ethical attitudes which that brought in train: we will hardly take seriously Paul's injunction, 'I mean brethren, the appointed time has grown very short; from now on, let those who have wives live as though they had none....' (1 Cor. 7:29).

Some have found the difficulties of the task of interpretation so overwhelming that they have abandoned any hope of recourse to the Bible. That is a counsel of despair. The Bible is our heritage, the book of the community, the food of life for the ordinary Christian, not the preserve of specialists. Many are naturals in the art of Christian discernment. The specialist tries to analyse what is happening in such authentic discernment and points to the need for a broad critical awareness—not only of the text but of the referent of the text, of the world which opens out before the text and the cultural horizon of that world, of the variety of literary genres with their contrast and complementarity, of the presuppositions (theological and other) that are likely to have influenced the authors.

One is increasinlgy aware also—and here in particular grass roots liberation movements have sharpened our thinking—of the need for a critical awareness of oneself, of one's own questions and presuppositions, of one's biases not only of a cultural and linguistic but also of a social, economic, political and sexual kind. It is possible to find support in the Bible for all sorts of activity: texts have a life of their own and will bear a variety of interpretations; they have been and continue to be appealed to in support of oppression, injustice and privilege. We now have a healthy suspicion that open-mindedness and neutrality in approach to the revelation—to discovering what God is saying to us—is much more elusive than we had thought and that there is required something that is a matter of heart and not just of historico-critical method. All our moves are not deductions from the Bible to the reality of the day. It may be that sympathetic openness to the reality is the key to what the age-old Bible is talking about. It may be that it is only an advocacy stance in relation to the obvious injustices of our time that will dispel our own blindness and sharpen our sense of the ideologies that have affected both the biblical writers and their interpreters through the ages. Only then can we be disciples of the text, free of our own ego and with a new capacity for knowing ourselves. Only then can there be genuine conversation back and forward with the text.

CHRISTIAN DISCERNMENT

One who enters the world-view of the Bible will, I believe, receive not just encouragement and motivation for moral life in general and for its particularities—and there is not space to develop that important issue—but *light* on judgment. One's religious world-view, one's faith, determines to some extent one's meanings, what for one are the facts of life (stories are facts) and what among them are the most relevant and significant facts. If that is so (Romans 12:2 suggests that Christians have a new mind or a new vision of reality) then we must allow that to be authoritative for us. It seems to me that faith has something to say, however subtly, about concepts that are the common coin of the moralist—good, welfare, happiness, flourishing, wholeness, rights, fairness, fulfilment. This is not to suggest that one cannot achieve an admirable morality outside of this context: part of my Christian story is about the goodness of creation and the validity of human thought and endeavour. But the Christian has to be fully true to him/herself. The challenge for the Christian is to discern in the light of or in the atmosphere of this total vision, to shape a character and life that are consonant with it, that pursue the ends and ideals that arise out of it. This will incorporate most of the great interpersonal values that are the heritage of the race as a whole—justice, respect, benevolence, equality, impartiality. But Christianity has its own perspective too and I want to look now at some of its prominent features.

For Christians as a class there is an enlarged reality in which there are values and meanings that may not exist for the non-Christian and which, for example, relativise secular notions of welfare, success and failure. This applies to judgment both about what Christians should seek for themselves and what they should seek for others: the most urgent need of the neighbour, Karl Barth said, is God himself. Knowledge of God, awareness of him, friendship with him is for the Christian the supreme good: attention to it may well modify one's attitude to goods which a non-believer regards as important. The justification of the Christian's life is suprahistorical and what appears to others as limitations on welfare or development may be regarded by the Christian as creative self-development.

One follows this line of thought into Christian traditions about detachment and trust. While there is in general Judaeo-Christian tradition a belief that God's world is good and a suggestion of a pro-attitude to it—in contrast with dualist or apocalyptic views—there are attitudes that derive from faith and that are summed up in the biblical injunction to be in the world but not of it or not to be anxious for tomorrow. It is true that one finds God in and through the human but one should so conduct oneself in human affairs as not to forget divine things. One should if need be sacrifice human development to progress in the divine. One may even renounce the normal human goods, e.g. marriage, family, friendship, society, as virgins and hermits have done, for the sake of the divine.

Likewise poverty of life and spirit is part of the Christian tradition. While much of secular moral literature is based on concepts of interest and desires, on one's right to a fair share of the available goods, Christians understand the spirit of the Gospels as saying that concern for the total meaning of one's life implies a certain kind of poverty in the pursuit of one's interests and that the way of radical poverty—of leaving all for the sake of the kingdom so as to accentuate the religious dimension and one's wider sense of blessedness—may be an intelligible choice. Not pressing one's claim is related both to personal creativity and to one's response to others. The Bible tells us that we are to seek the interests of others and not our own, that we are to give to everyone who asks, wash one another's feet, forgive enemies, be prepared to lay down our lives for the neighbour. This curious asymmetry in relationships seems to be the logic of a faith that has stories about the forgiving love of God for us, about a Saviour who died for us when we were yet sinners, about the final and total meaning of our lives.

There is talk in Christianity too about bearing the cross. It is not a matter of opting out, of cowardice or weakness. It is that the experience of Jesus, and especially his death-resurrection, has something to say to every human being. Moral literature generally seems to envisage situations of logic and clarity in which we are dealing with perfectly reasonable people. But we live in a world in which justice will not be done, in which rights will not be allowed, in which goodness will not be rewarded, in which evil prospers. A fair slice of life is about injustice and about situations which have injustice written into them. We must struggle for justice for ourselves and others, but in situations where we do not or are not likely to obtain it there must also be a Christian response: it cannot be a response that is divorced from the stories and symbols that are the very stuff of Christianity. It is interesting that there is a strong tradition of non-violence in Christianity.

Hanging over the Christian's discernment in the broadest sense is the central belief in an intelligent and loving God who is creator and last end. In the most general sense this shapes one's attitudes to oneself, to others and even to the inanimate world. It determines the perspective from which one sees reality: it gives a certain kind of metaphysic. 'The earth is the Lord's and the fulness thereof, the world and those who dwell therein' (Ps. 24). 'None of us lives to himself. . . . If we live, we live to the Lord. . . . ' (Rom. 14:7-8). No one is a favourite before God: those who do the will of the Father are brothers and sisters of the Lord; there must be no room for personal rivalry or vanity (Mk. 3:35; Phil. 2:3). Whatever we have we have in stewardship: all is under the creative plan and purposes of God. Such considerations suggest a certain style of life—a respect for all, a modesty and humility of mien and behaviour.

These are a few of the general thrusts of the biblical world-view. They are the kinds of attitude and judgment that are elusively suggested by biblical sayings about the one thing necessary, about losing and finding one's life, taking up the cross, taking no thought for tomorrow, regarding others as better than oneself, seeking not one's own rights but those of others, laying down one's life, rejoicing in mourning and persecution. They are the background to the paradoxical language of the Sermon on the Mount. They do not and are not meant to tell us exactly what to do. They are not precise directives but thrusts for living that grow out of how one regards oneself and one's world in Christ. They must enter

58

into Christian discernment: how they will do so is up to each individual to decide.

Can one be moral without the Bible? Obviously. Is recourse to the Bible possible? Yes, difficult but possible. Does a Christian need it for a full appreciation of Christian moral life? I think so. What I have outlined is, I suppose, the Christian ideal but it is difficult to see that anything less qualifies as Christian moral thinking. Moral life is not just about basic right and wrong. It is more satisfactorily seen as an ideal or perfection to be realised. It calls for Christian character—the ability to choose and live in accordance with a settled Christian vision and disposition. It is true that Catholic moral theology once made a sharp distinction between command and counsel and that the philosophical tradition made much of the distinction between duty and supererogation (i.e. what goes beyond strict duty)—so much so that some elements of it did not even admit ideals under the rubric of morality. But the philosophical tradition is now much more open to the notion of character and Catholic moral theology can be said to have abandoned the distinction of command and counsel. Vatican II laid it down that the basic vocation is that of baptism and that this calls all to the following of Christ. It is more helpful to envisage morality on a scalar model and certainly it is hard to see that the NT community was ready to recommend anything lower on the scale than life in the likeness of Jesus Christ who lived love to the end.

So when the Christian asks the kind of question with which we opened this chapter—what am I do do? what is right or wrong for me?—a responsible answer is one that arises out of the biblical ethos-ethic. We are to make our judgments in fidelity to our total story. This is not to advocate some esoteric discernment. There need be no blurring of the discipline of moral science. Christian morality need not collapse in a fog of pious sentiment. The Christian facts of life to which I refer are public facts—at least for those who subscribe to Christian faith. If there is a 'faith-instinct' in moral matters (Rahner) I take that to be the fruit of the stories, symbols, aims and intentions that are our particular heritage—of which the Bible is the classic and indispensable statement. About the bearing of such on moral judgment the Christian should be able to give some account.

Is there a specifically Christian morality? This is hardly a matter of primary importance. Christians should not feel any compulsion to prove a special morality. On the other hand there is no need to apologise for doing morality in fidelity to one's world-view. Everybody does so. There is no position of pure rationality that is uncontaminated by metaphysical presuppositions: the atheist or agnostic position is not 'pure'. What is needed is that Christians do their morality in line with their story. Whether and to what extent this gives them a morality that is specific, i.e. peculiar to Christianity and different from all other moralities, depends on a number of considerations. It depends, first, on the term of comparison. There are obviously some world-views that are more sympathetic to and more in harmony with the Christian world-view than others. It also depends on what one regards as the domain of the moral—are acts directed to God, acts of worship for example, part of morality as Catholicism has traditionally regarded them? Are vocational choices of poverty, chastity and obedience part of it? Is the judgment made in faith that one is called and enabled to give one's life for another part of it? I think so.

Again, how easily can one delimit what we have called the content of morality? Can one separate content from what some Catholic authors have called motive e.g. the motive that enters into choices of self-sacrifice, celibacy, poverty, trust, detachment? Does the motive not determine the description of the act, of what is being chosen, of the content of the act? Does the manner of performing actions enter into morality—one's intention, disposition, attachments, innermost desires, sentiments? I would argue that they do. The more attention is given to such considerations the more likely is the claim that there is a specific Christian morality—since morality will include not only what is done but why and how. For example, it matters why one chooses to be detached, poor, self-sacrificing, celibate, accepting of suffering etc. The more morality is understood in terms of character and virtue, therefore, the more one can speak of something specific.

However, one wonders if Christians should spend much energy in proving specificity. There will be considerable areas of agreement between Christian and non-Christian—between all who have a concern for the person, for rights, justice, fairness and benevolence—particularly at the level of material norms or negative rules. But it needs to be pointed out nevertheless that one cannot catch all of morality in such norms. The moral vocation is dynamic and open-ended. It is highly personal. It requires that one respond to individual situations with responsibility and imagination. The task of the Christian community is to recall and celebrate the Christian story so that it actively informs our lives today. The task of Christian moral science is to delineate the vision and the thrusts that are consonant with Christian faith. The task of moral education is to encourage the emergence of character that in the variety of human situations will know how to allow faith to bear on choice in continuity with the great tradition which we have inherited.

4

THE TRUTH IN LOVE

IF there is one thrust or recommendation that stands out in
the ethos-ethic of the Bible it is that of neighbour-love, what
the New Testament calls agape. The Synoptics with Paul and
John all give it a prominent place and it has become a constant
of the Christian tradition that Christians are to love others.
The position of love has become more pronounced in Catholic
moral theology in recent decades. Time was when love (or
charity) was regarded as just one of many moral responses
required of us. It had its own tract—not very substantial—tucked away in the moral theology text book among
more impressive treatments of the Commandments—do not
kill or steal or commit adultery. In recent decades there has
been an effort to bring it centre stage. Some moral theologians
refer to the primacy or centrality of love in Christian life. They
regard it as the fundamental principle of morality—and the
search for one root-principle which grounds and holds
together all moral life has always been a concern of moralists.
They see it as the justification of all moral rules. And they see
all morality as some expression of it. This seems to correspond
to the instinct of Christians generally. If you ask people what
Christian morality is about they are likely to reply that it is
about love.

There is much debate about what agape means and this
chapter will try to examine the notion. For the moment I
propose that we accept as a working definition that it means at
least a concern for all human beings—including oneself—a disposition to seek their good and an active engagement to
promote that. Some such stance seems to me to be the heart of
morality. I mean that a recognition of a claim of the other on
us—and of the need to take one's own being seriously—is the

core of moral experience: that this claim is the basis of the moral point of view: and that moral living is the attempt to order one's life in accordance with it. The task of the moral community then is to discover the expression of neighbour-love and to enable human beings to align their lives with it.

There is no question here of saying that such concern is specific to Christianity or that one needs to be a Christian in order to recognise or live it. Our concern as Christians is not to make comparisons with other systems but to be faithful to our own vision. We all know that non-Christians love their fellow human beings—indeed some of them claim that their love is more genuine than the love of religious people.

It is well to recognise also that many philosophical systems are based on concern for others. For example there are systems that are explicitly based on respect for others, on benevolence towards others, on the golden rule of doing to others as we would have them do to us, or on some system of the rights of others. Indeed it has been explicitly claimed that the notion of agape coincides precisely with one or other of these theories. Some have thought that it is exactly the same as the theory of respect for persons, or as the golden rule, or as the Kantian principle that one should treat others as ends and never merely as a means, or as the utilitarian principle of doing the greatest good.

I am not contending that biblical agape is a higher form of morality than such philosophical systems. One would need to sort out many moral notions before that question could even be approached—for example, one's position on the relation of duty and supererogation, of command and counsel. (Biblical agape does indeed hold out a very high ideal of love, even to the laying down of one's life for others, but one needs to ask in what way the Christian community sees this as a *demand* or requires it.) Although Christians talk a lot about agape we have to acknowledge that the very meaning of a moral theory of agape is not clear. It may well be that those authors are correct who say that it falls under one of the well-known philosophical theories or some combination of them. It seems reasonable to ask at any rate that it be able to determine its position with respect to such well-worn theories. It would be naive to regard it as a simple theory which can be easily applied to the complexity of human life and that can escape the difficulties which have been found to attend all theories that are based on concern for the person. In choosing to look at agape as the central moral theory for Christians I am aware, then, that I will be covering ground that is not specific to Christianity but can be equally claimed by much philosophical morality.

THE BIBLE AND AGAPE

We refer rather freely to the biblical teaching on agape. But the biblical teaching is various. The most obvious source is the double commandment in Matthew 22:39, Mark 12:31, Luke 10:27 (cf. Mt. 5:43, 19:19 and Jn. 13:34). But the belief that agape should characterise the Christian life does not depend on a command of Jesus. Nor is New Testament teaching on agape necessarily tied to the actual incidence of the word 'agape'. In Paul it is the whole kerygma that forms the basis of the demand, i.e. the whole story of the loving initiative of God in our regard. Agape-love is seen as a response to the very nature of God in his redemptive activity: it arises out of gratitude for God's grace; it is a gift of the Spirit; it should be—especially forgiving love—the attitude of one who has been forgiven by God (cf. Rom. 3:21; 2 Cor. 4:4 and 5:14; Gal. 4:4; Col. 3:13). The same dynamic appears in John. Love, John says, is of God. He has first loved us and we ought to love one another (1 Jn. 4:10-11): Christ has laid down his life for us and we ought to lay down our lives for one another (1 Jn. 3:16). The same themes appear in the Synoptics. The Father is generous and merciful, his concern is sovereign and spontaneous. He shows kindness to those who despise him. This spontaneous love (Mt. 5:45; Lk. 6:35) is the basis for agape, and especially for love of enemies: the Christian should love as the Father loves, without expecting a return, giving blessing for cursing and praying for his persecutors (Mt. 5:44, Lk. 6:27, 35).

So New Testament agape is active. It is for all. It is to be in the likeness of God and of Christ. It includes enemies and even the laying down of life for the other. It is, as John in particular insists, a commandment for the Christians of the last times, a sign of true knowledge of God and of belonging to the community of light, a sign of credibility for the Church, a continuation of the love of the Father for the Son and of the Son for the disciples. Within this rather diffused teaching on agape there is room for two interpretations of the essence of love. Some regard it as pure bestowal without any consideration of the worth of the other, sovereign, unmotivated save by the necessity to be itself—in the likeness of God whose love is not determined, it is said, by any human worth but is sheer graciousness. Others include at least some element of appraisal: the other is to be loved because he/she has worth, perhaps additionally because of such worth in relation to God.

Obviously there are a great variety of relationships between one person and another and much work has gone into sorting out the different experiences that might pass as love. The medievals spoke of the love of desire (*amor concupiscentiae*), the love of benevolence (*amor benevolentiae*) and the love of friendship (*amor amicitiae*). C. S. Lewis distinguished need-love and gift-love and identified four experiences: affection, friendship, eros and charity.[1] There has been a considerable literature on the distinction between agape (regarded as an unselfish love of others) and eros (containing at least some element of selfish desire and satisfaction).[2] Philosophers and theologians are putting words on our experiences. We are all aware of the complexity and subtlety of our experiences of relatedness. In the midst of that complexity we recognise that one can, roughly speaking, distinguish between love relationships that are predominantly self-centred and those that are predominantly other-centred. We know that our motives and dispositions are usually mixed and we often cannot determine the exact mixture of selfishness and unselfishness.

It may even be that it pays us to have regard for others and to develop institutions that ensure such regard. Even theories of morality explicitly based on self-interest find it necessary to propose altruistic considerations—as the best way to provide for one's self-interest. It has been maintained, for example, that the best way to ensure our own security is to enter into some kind of contract, implicit or explicit, with others—otherwise we might all be wolves towards one another. It is clear that such systems do not meet the demands of New Testament agape, that indeed what the New Testament is proposing is at the unselfishness end of the spectrum of love. We are to be like the Father who blesses those who curse him and like Christ who died for us when we were sinners. We are to bless those who revile us and pray for our persecutors. In an early Christian document, the Didache, the command to love is given along with a promise that then 'you will have no enemy'. But in the New Testament this expectation is lacking and the command stands without any promise attached to it. (Lk. 6:28, cf. Rom. 12:14, 1 Cor. 4:12).

A DEFINITION: REGARD AND COMMITMENT

We stand in a great variety of relationships to one another—friend, spouse, neighbour, parent, child, colleague, employer, employee, companion. All of these relationships have their own form, tone and contour. Yet the New Testament suggests that one word can somehow cover all of them, can indicate a valid fundamental stance. If that is so it must be a word that has a basic meaning but that is capable of taking on a rich variety of nuances. Could we look then at a proposed definition. This is Gene Outka's : 'Agape is a regard for the neighbour which in crucial respects is independent and unalterable. To these features there is a corollary: the regard is for every person qua human existent, to be distinguished from those special traits, actions etc. which distinguish particular personalities from each other.... One ought to be committed to the other's well-being independently and unalterably; and to view the other as irreducibly valuable prior to his doing anything in particular.'[3] I think I am happy with this.

Regard for the other
One can readily see the central importance of the triad of terms, 'human existent', 'irreducibly valuable', 'independent and unalterable'. I want in this section to develop two other elements—regard and commitment to well-being. Regard says something about attitude or disposition towards the other. Minimally it seems to point to a respect for the other. It is, I suppose, compatible with a certain natural antipathy. We know perfectly well that there are some people whom we naturally like and others with whom, for a great variety of reasons, we do not experience any natural sympathy. We can hope to be able to reduce the number in the latter category—and that is indeed possible—but we will hardly be likely to eliminate it completely. Psychologists increasingly tell us to acknowledge such feelings of antipathy and not pretend

to ourselves that we have a natural liking for everybody. We must still try to love all. Agape-love appears to require of us an appreciation of every other, some sense of reverence based on the fact of his/her being a human being, some sisterly or brotherly feeling. It requires that we attend at least to the obvious fact of common humanity and refuse to ignore it, whatever the temptations, whatever the natural antipathy, allowing it rather to impinge on us with its claim. This regard or sympathy has a natural comcomitant in action but it is not yet action. It refers to something that comes before action, that will accompany and issue in action.

I am making a point here about the importance of motive and disposition in morality—of virtue and character. It is obvious that we can perform beneficent acts towards others for a great variety of motives. Giving material help to persons in need will look like an act of love. But I can give material help to them in order to patronise them, to humiliate them, because I am afraid of them or others, because I have been ordered to do so by an authority, or in order that others may see me and praise me—all without any regard. (The analysis of motive is an interesting study.) *What* I did cannot be described without some attention to *why* I did it (I may indeed have done it from mixed motives). What I did in the instances cited here was not an act of love: that seems obvious. Look at it even in terms of duty and you will find that this is not entirely satisfactory either. I can do my duty to others—I can give them what they need and what I may be in duty bound to give. It is something. It may even be much. It may be more than many give who talk much of love and do nothing. So the one who acts out of a sense of duty is not to be undervalued. But he/she has some distance to go in order to act as the New Testament expects. Doing what is good for others is not necessarily loving them. Love is a virtue of attachment as well as of action and the disposition of the heart is part of the virtue. Perhaps there are several degrees within that disposition from the beginning of charity to its perfection.

One must not underestimate this regard for others. It is a difficult stance to have and to have it as a permanent disposition and with regard to all others is something of a miracle. We seem to be naturally enclosed in ourselves. We want to establish ourselves, to pursue and get what builds us up and satisfies us. That is the native thrust of all of us. To let some other dynamic, some other mode of life, operate is difficult. To accept the otherness of the other—that each other exists for him/herself with similar desires and hopes and a similar destiny to our own—is a shift of consciousness. Even to treat others equally and impartially with ourselves, to do to them as we would have them do to us, to recognise in practice that the other in no way exists for us and is not to be subordinated to us, is difficult. To go beyond it to a position of positive altruistic regard is greater still: it is a real conversion.

And yet it is interrelatedness that is the key issue for us. It is a piece of ancient Eastern wisdom that where there are others there is dread: we see them as threat rather than as gift. It is in the resolution of this that the fundamental drama of our lives is lived out and that in the end our response to God is given or refused—'as you did it not to one of the least of these you did it not to me'. It is only when we accept the community of others and recognise our responsibility to them that our own humanness becomes possible. That requires of us a shift from a perspective and purpose in life in which the only thing of value is our own plans to one in which the welfare of others becomes a significant part of that purpose. Somewhere within us we know that. If only we could get in touch with that deeper self and let it sing to us. Sheer forcing or willing does not bring about the conversion; we can only hope and pray for it and meantime perhaps try to identify in our psyche the factors which inhibit it.

Commitment to the Good or Well-being of the Other

Agape then requires both other-regard, i.e. a disposition to have certain feelings and thoughts, and a readiness to do certain actions in relation to the other. So the second element in Outka's definition is the 'commitment to the other's well-being'. Agape cannot remain merely an attitude or a way of perceiving the other. As we saw, New Testament love is active and the New Testament community indicated several of the implications or concrete demands of love. The tradition has rendered this by saying that love requires that we seek the good or welfare of the other—and of ourselves.

How human good or welfare is to be interpreted we will look at in a moment. What is immediately obvious is that agape-love is being related here to what one does. I take 'do to others' in a very broad sense to cover the great variety of ways in which one affects another. It will mean not only doing something but also doing nothing. At times it will mean being silently supportive, staying with or suffering with another. To say that it involves the welfare of the other means that it is to be judged by the manner in which it issues in or affects others. It is not merely a matter of what I, the agent, feel, of my intention, of the desire or emotion with which I do something. What happens to the other or what I intend to happen is crucial. There are actions that cannot count as loving because of their effect on the other—however I feel about such actions. We saw that the performance of a loving act depends on me in the sense that it involves my mental disposition. But what pieces of behaviour can be realistically and really intended as loving does not depend on me but on what in actual fact contributes to someone's welfare. I may say that I meant something as an act of love or intended it as such or that I did it out of love. That—if it is genuine—is highly important and is obviously vastly different from an act that is done out of hatred, envy or other evil intent. But it is not enough if I did not go to the trouble to discover whether or not it is likely to issue in the welfare of the other. Even to mean well will not do: the best will in the world may produce the worst results in the world; harm can be done not only by evil agents but by those who do not go to the trouble to calculate the way of love. It may be difficult at times to determine what are the acts of love but what I am maintaining is that there are such, that they can be brought under the notion of 'welfare' and that we must exercise our minds and hearts about them. Discovering what love requires will demand from us sympathy, sensitivity and imagination.

When we refer to the good or welfare of others we are using 'good' in a *non-moral, pre-moral* or factual sense. Since the idea will recur in this book it is well to note it. What do we mean by human, pre-moral or non-moral good? I think the meaning is caught by expressions such as 'good for you' and 'do you good'. In referring to pre-moral good one is not saying anything yet about morality or about what one ought to do. But, as we shall see, pre-moral good—what is good for you—has huge implications for morality. Because morality is about doing (human or pre-moral) good to others, doing to or for them what is good for them. This gives us a chance once again to take some of the mystery out of morality. An understanding of morality is not a matter of knowledge of arcane laws that is the preserve of a few. It is an understanding of what is good for people. We all have ideas about that. If we do, we can discuss morality. We should have views about it: it is within our grasp.

So your mother might tell you that vegetables are good for you or that it will do you good to eat your lunch or that fresh air is good for you or exercise or moderation or getting up early in the morning. We have a wide range of things that we commonly refer to as good for us—good food, a good environment, a sunny summer, a well-run school, education in the arts, a range of virtues. There is some underlying notion here of things which, we believe, will bring us some sense of—of what? I think some sense of well-being, wholeness, flourishing, fulfilment, satisfaction. There is implied a notion of incompletion, potential, movement, desire. Desire is basic to life. We are always looking for things—everything we do is done because we expect that we will feel or be better as a result. So we aspire to states which we are not in at the moment: we can describe our relation to the objects (taken in a very wide sense) that can bring about such states by saying that they are values for us. As we say, we value them.

We turn our attention to the notion of desire for the next few paragraphs. What we want to tease out is the relation of welfare—and therefore of love—to the fulfilment of our own desires and those of others. We desire things in different ways. We campaign to have fresh air or a non-polluted atmosphere for the sake of health. We desire a good educational system so that we may have knowledge and a sense of adult autonomy. We work hard because we desire to have enough money to go on holidays to Spain where we believe we will have a great sense of enjoyment or satisfaction. In a different sort of way we desire courage so as to be able to do what we should do when the need arises. We say that we desire perfect happiness—full stop.

Good and Desires
Would you say that loving others means giving them what

they desire? Or that true love of yourself means getting your desires? The question is whether having desires fulfilled is good for human beings. We link welfare and the satisfaction of desires presumably because we believe that people know and desire what is good for them. But perhaps desire is not a helpful clue to welfare. On the other hand it seems odd to say that something is for a person's welfare or well-being if he/she experiences no satisfaction from it. There are few things that people resent so much as being told by others that something is for their good when they do not feel that in any way. Perhaps the moral problem is one of learning to find satisfaction in what is truly good for us.

We have to acknowledge that the satisfaction of our desires does not always contribute to our well-being—whereas something may contribute to it which we do not currently desire. So children are sent to school often against their wishes. Young people are advised to refrain from drugs. We are all told not to abandon ourselves to drink or pleasure, etc. Some of this is a matter of experience, of learning what we truly desire. We know that we have in the past desired things that did not in fact lead to well-being. We agree that we would have been better off without them: they turn to ashes in our mouths and leave us feeling worse off rather than better. Even apart from consulting our experience we can sometimes take the long view and find that our long-term desires are incompatible with our short-term ones: e.g. desires for brief and passing pleasures are incompatible with some other kind of more deeply desired condition of which we are in some way conscious. We also find that others have a well-founded belief—from their knowledge of us or of human beings generally and from the wisdom of the race—that what we now desire will not in fact lead to our well-being. We often hear the remark, 'You do not know what is good for you'. Parents, for example, often act in the hope that their children will recognise afterwards that what they proposed was what was best—was indeed what they (the children) would have desired if they had known better.

Most people like to think that they know what is best for them. How can others tell them what they would desire if they were wise and fully informed—about their own affairs? How can parents, for example, say it to their children? Is there some accumulated human wisdom about this? Do all people

71

fundamentally and prudently desire some nameable goods, states or conditions of life—or would they if they were more informed, more humanly developed or more sensitised? There are those who believe that some things are so generally and basically desired that one is justified in using a stronger word for them—needs. Would you be prepared to say that you desire certain basic things and that all others whom you have met also desire them at some level, so that one can speak of basic human needs? If so, one must be attentive to the very wide range of needs: human nature and human psychology are extremely complex and the variety of ways in which human beings find fulfilment is correspondingly large.

The matter becomes more acute if we think of cross-cultural situations. There is variation in desire from culture to culture and we are being told repeatedly not to come with our own agenda to another culture but to listen to the needs of those in the culture. The more we study the matter probably the less we can say about common desires or needs. But even here there are some things that can be said. Do people generally want to lose their lives? Most seem to try hard not to; why else the struggle for human rights or the massive efforts to combat famine and poverty. Most people seem to want independence: they want to throw off the shackles of dependence or slavery in order to organise their own lives and participate in their own structures. Most want respect, love, fellowship. It is conceded now that some of this requires conscientisation. What does that mean? A heightening of awareness? But of what? Apparently of the basic needs which people in all cultures have, even though, because of exploitation or oppression, they are currently only dimly aware of them and do not actively desire them.

More than Desires?

It may well be that the desires of others are a guide to what is their good and therefore to what loving them involves. We do well to listen closely to what people are saying about their needs—however softly or obscurely they are saying it. But it is not easy to work solely with the notion of desire and it may be that welfare can only with difficulty be brought under the rubric of desire. We recognise that the fulfilment even of prudent desires—unless perhaps 'desire' is understood, as we shall see, in a very deep sense—is not always what is best for people. We would not be doing justice to how we experience ourselves in the world if we did not note that. We have a sense that certain courses are appropriate even though we cannot easily be said to desire them. We recognise this, I say: it is a demand of ourselves, a requirement of being faithful to ourselves as human beings. The human race has known this for a long time. Plato tells us that it is better—i.e. it is good for us—to suffer injustice than to cause it, even though it might be more profitable to cause it and we might well desire to revenge the injustice. Aristotle tells us that wealth, which is so much desired, has brought ruin to many, has destroyed them. We do not need to be told, we have all seen it. How do we mean 'destroyed'? How do we mean 'brought to ruin'? Ruin to what? There is some notion here that what the person desired and sought is not his/her welfare or well-being, not where his/her true good lies. (Just last night I saw a man declare on television, 'Certainly I drink more than I should'.) There is therefore a welfare that does not easily fall under the notion of desire but that is nevertheless well recognised by us.

It has to do, I think, with the fact that we are beings of a certain kind or nature and that out life has an inbuilt harmony. Our talk about our true good and about being true to ourselves is a recognition that there are choices and acts that *fit*—because they correspond to what we are and lead to our being more fully human. These are not discovered by focusing on desires. The pursuit of our own current desires and the satisfaction of the desires of others may well be appropriate. But they are not decisive. I know, for example, that it is good for me to receive affirmation, esteem and good food—all of which I desire. I know also that it is good for me to be just, sober and moderate, to respect and take account of others, to be unselfish, to look after my health, to make room for prayer etc. even though perhaps I do not currently desire any of these things and, as I am now, could not even imagine myself actually desiring them. We know it, I say. There really is no way of proving or illustrating this except by appealing to our total experience of ourselves: at least in flashes we recognise that such are part of our good.

So we have to say that love of ourselves is not just a matter of seeking our desires. Being loved is not just a matter of having our desires met. Love of others is not necessarily a matter of granting their desires. That is to put it bluntly. But we have to go gently with our own lives and those of others. There is a sensible gradualism about moral life: what and how much anyone can take or give at a particular moment is to be delicately assessed. I shall have more to say about that in Chapter 6.

It is here that most of us experience the tension of moral life. Often, there appears to be a conflict between what we desire and what morality calls us to—in my terms between what we desire and what is good for us. We tend to relate to others in a way that satisfies our desires. We want others to grant our desires and we often find it easiest to grant theirs—whether it is good for them or not. Morality appears as a kill-joy—you know the remark that anything that is worthwhile in life is either fattening, illegal or immoral.

Or Deeper Desires?

Some thinkers try to resolve the tension by suggesting that we retain here the notion of desire or want. Their contention is that if we really understood ourselves we would see that we do desire at a very deep level what is our true and real good and that this is what is implied when we say that we want true happiness. They suggest that we have an inner sense of this true good—as appears from a few paragraphs back—and a thrust towards it. So that loving others and oneself—being moral—is not a matter of going against our desires but of seeking what we most want (and giving others what they most want) even if it is not what we currently want. A sign of this deep desire and thrust is the peace which we experience when we follow—often at some cost—what we know to be our good. It is not surprising if it is so: it is to be expected that we would find true harmony in listening to the promptings of our deepest desires. This, I suppose, could be seen as a further version of the notion of being wise and fully informed which we considered a few pages back. But it is at a much deeper level. And it is not just a matter of information, of head, but of heart. Where is our heart: in what direction do our affections habitually lie; how open are we to our deepest self?

The idea that our welfare lies in doing what we want is an attractive one. But our problem is in acknowledging and being attracted by this deeper wanting, in getting in touch with our whole selves. We experience several levels of wanting. I want to be an upright politician but I also want to keep my seat. I want to make right decisions but I also want to be thought a nice guy by everybody. I want to be a patient spouse but I also have a little desire to get even with a partner who has hurt me. I want to be just but I also want that holiday in Spain which I can get by deceiving my employer or employees. I want reconciliation in Northern Ireland but I also want old scores settled. I want fairness and impartiality for all but I also want to be king of the castle. So much so that it is hard to recognise what is good for me: the beaches in Spain loom large and seem to be the only thing worth pursuing; the fantasy of power or of seeing my oppressors humiliated exercises a powerful pull. Mere desire—and often pre-rational desires—and feeling cloud my judgment. Discernment of what is my genuine good—health, integration, the virtues of justice, fairness, impartiality, forgiveness etc.—is in danger of being distorted so that I may judge what is not truly good to be the best option for me, the thing worth pursuing. And in the name of love I can blackmail others into giving it to me.

There is much in the ethos-ethic of the New Testament about this central tension of living. It warns us against filling our barns, seeking the first places, winning men's favour, wanting to lord it over others. It has paradoxical things to say about losing and finding one's life, one's true self. The Sermon on the Mount has a philosophy which overturns our accepted pattern of desires—striving, seeking and possessing. It holds out tantalising promises that blessedness and wholeness are found in quite the opposite direction. But such blessedness, I suspect, is not found by a cold obedience to directives from without—St Thomas Aquinas tells us that the law of the new covenant is not found even in the prescriptions of the New Testament—but in allowing to emerge our full and true selves which have been overlaid by our frenetic efforts to establish ourselves with security and surround ourselves with the approval of others.

> And the end of all our exploring
> Will be to arrive where we started
> And know the place for the first time.
> (T. S. Eliot, *Little Gidding*)

75

Much of our lives is a struggle between these different levels of wanting. It is possible to pursue what we glimpse to be our true good even when our desires and inclinations are strongly in another direction. But it is difficult. What we know to be the true good for us may not bring satisfaction. We can still seek it, clinging to our beliefs. But life is not fully lived, we have not reached true humanity until such choice and such a way of life are *experienced* as good for us, until there is some joy and satisfaction in the choice. That suggests that moral life might be thought of as a matter of education, of educating our desires—to want what is truly good and to find some joy in pursuing it. How to educate them is the problem. It is not just a matter of will-power: it is a growth in sensibility.

Let us try to sum up what I have been saying in this chapter. I want to say two things. First, that there are states, conditions and objects the pursuit or achievement of which can be said to be good for human beings: they make for their wholeness or well-being. That I am proposing as a matter of fact. Second, that we recognise that it is intelligent to treat others and behave ourselves in a manner that helps to achieve that well-being—and that any other basic stance does not make sense. At least it does not make sense to one who has a developed awareness of what it means to be a human person and who is able to judge about life and its choices in accordance with that. That is what I mean by saying that love is a fundamental moral stance. So love is care and regard. But like the love of God for us, it is a care and regard that are truly creative, that enable and empower the other to be and to be fully—and that are free enough and wise enough to be able to do that.

Refusal

What if one does not desire what is good for him/herself and others—one's sense of the only worthwhile pursuit in life may be wealth, pleasure or power? That is a pity. One is out of harmony with the truth for living, with whole human understanding and response. What if one knows the true way but cannot harness the energy to follow one's perception? That too is a pity. One has not mastered the art of being a human being. One is not an artist at living. One has not carved out of the raw material of life the beautiful object that can be carved. One is falling short of the ideal human being. It was in such terms that

76

the Greeks and the great medievals thought, and perhaps we also might think thus of moral life, of the moral 'ought' and of moral obligation rather than in terms of some law that is imposed on us from without. The moral call is a call to be a human being. Moral failure is a failure to be such. Moral obligation is the awareness of a fundamental and intelligible thrust in that direction. Morality is a matter of listening to and nurturing the invitation within to be fully ourselves by our openness to others. If we do refer to the requirements of moral life as law we might think of them as the directives which some master craftsman would indicate who understood perfectly what it means to be human.

WORKING OUT THE DETAILS: LOVE, VALUES AND RULES

What then are we to do for others and seek for ourselves? It should be possible to go some distance in spelling out what human welfare involves. Life is varied, bounteous and complex and the demands of right living will be as varied as the possibilities of human wholeness or flourishing—what we see as values for us. Thus life and health are good and so a healthy atmosphere is good for us. Knowledge, psychic well-being, independence, a sense of responsibility are good and so a sound social and educational system is important. Self-esteem and friendship are good and so the ability to mix socially and a happy upbringing and family life are good. Honourable disposition, generosity of spirit are good and so a healthy moral environment is good. Rootedness is good and so a sense of one's culture is good. Sensitivity to beauty is good and so a rich cultural environment is good. Union with God is good and so the availability of religious faith is good. It is maintained by some—as we shall see in the next chapter—that these can be reduced to a number of core goods. Again I mean by 'good' what factually makes for human growth and wholeness. I am not saying that they are self-evidently good or that they appear good to all—we have already seen problems about that. But I am saying that most of them (there are obvious problems about religious values but I have given some hints in the last chapter about how one might view that question) are perceived as good by those who are able to open themselves to what it means to be a human being.

Many people would agree that such goods or goals at the broadest level are worth pursuing. So we have some general ideas of the direction of moral action—it is in the direction of respect for life, care for its handing on and nurture, the provision of education. It is in the direction of seeking the truth, allowing others to seek it, not denying it to them. It is in the direction of ensuring freedom. It is in the direction of trust, fidelity and social harmony. These statements do not specify exactly the piece of behaviour that counts as loving or moral. They have to be cashed in particular situations. But they are not empty: they indicate in a general way the style of right living.

But two points need to be made. The first is that different cultures might interpret differently how they are to be realised. Indeed it seems that in our own culture we are going through a phase of questioning some of our accepted ways of pursuing human goals. Doubts are often raised now about whether affluence is good for us, whether educational systems with their emphasis on competitiveness are truly human, whether economic development is humanly successful, whether development programmes in the Third World are not humanly counter-productive, whether technological progress is necessarily human progress, whether our ability to tame the environment is to our overall advantage, whether increased mobility is a boon. Whether, overall, our pursuit of many of these lines has not blinded us to what is our whole and genuine welfare. Certainly we have a long list of modern ills—stress, tension, drug dependence, alienation, the break-up of cultures, the poisoning of ourselves and of our environment—which makes us ask where we are going.

The second point is this. It is about moral rules—about what precisely is the way of love—that most controversy arises. The more general one remains in moral discourse the more agreement there will be. You are safe if you remain with the generalities of the second last paragraph. When one tries to state precisely what the welfare of ourselves and others requires of us—and that is what a moral rule does—one runs into difficulty. What is typical of rules is that they are not general but name the piece of behaviour that embodies love or does not. To provide for the handing on of life—for the future of the race—is, as we said in the second last paragraph, the right

78

direction of action. You will get wide agreement on that. But can one say that this also implies that only permanent and monogamous marriage is the right way for the procreation of children, the way of love. About that there will be less agreement. Our tradition has plenty of examples of such precise rules: it says that adultery, telling untruths, contraception, pre-marital sex, etc, are wrong, are not the way of love. There are problems about stating rules and we will have more to say about this in Chapter 7.

Individual and Community

The last four paragraphs have moved us a bit more into wider notions of welfare and in particular have raised questions about the relation of the individual and the community with its structures and institutions. That will occupy us more in the next chapter but we must look at it briefly here. We naturally begin by thinking about love in terms of the individual. It immediately brings up for us the problem of loving some particular person—spouse, child, parent, employer, employee, companion, colleague. We all realise how difficult it can be to know how to love another, to discern what his/her welfare requires at a particular time. We are often warned that judgments are sometimes more a reflection of our own need than that of the other—not only when we appear to be selfish but also when we appear to be unselfish. We know also how good decisions are inhibited by fear of the emotional mess that confrontation leaves. Once again, there is a certain freedom required in order to see situations truly.

A fair amount of our moral life has to do with this personal one-to-one relationship. But it is a primary fact that we live together in communities, that therefore love must be directed in several directions at the one time. Our lives are a tapestry of interwoven patterns. We find ourselves in many intersecting circles as parents, employees, managers, citizens, politicians, members of voluntary organisations etc. Acts which favour the welfare of one may deny a possibility to another or have a harmful effect on the totality. We have become more aware also in recent times of world-wide inter-dependence. Our action affects not only those near us, not only the particular society with which we identify but other societies far from us. We live in the global village. Our life-style, trade, financial dealings, all have implications for the welfare of those whom we have never met.

We cannot live as individuals. Neither can those to whom we would do good. It is obvious from the list of goods which we have mentioned that the good of the individual is heavily dependent on some more general well-being—on the well-being of some whole or community to which we belong (and we belong to several). To think of the well-being or flourishing of a community is presumably to think of a condition or state that facilitates or encourages the well-being of each one in that community. One might think of moral life then as playing one's part in the community in a way that facilitates its genuine growth. What is good for the community is not at odds with what is good for the individual—at least not necessarily. Often there will be no question about opposing them: we may spontaneously seek what is the good of the individual with whom we are concerned, without worrying about whether it cuts across the good of the wider community. So a doctor, parent, educator or friend will think in terms of the physical, moral, psychic, social or religious development of the person in front of them. But we also need to keep the perspective. It is not difficult to think of situations where to pursue the welfare, say the health, of one individual is at the expense of others. For example, there are difficult questions asked about how resources should be allocated—health, educational, cultural or economic.

Such questions will not be solved simply by thinking in terms of loving each individual. Many decisions are about who is to suffer, who is to be left out. In a general sort of way one will want to say that the good of the community will be primary, both because there are more people to be genuinely cared for and also because it is likely that acts, programmes and decisions that promote the physical, psychic, intellectual, cultural, moral and religious well-being of the community as a whole will, at least in the long term, be for the good of the individual next to me. This however leaves unanswered some serious questions about whether and to what extent an individual's good is to be subordinated to the whole. About this tension we will have something to say in the next chapter.

Love, Charity, Justice

Whatever about 'love', the word 'charity' has had a bad press. It is associated with almsgiving, with attempts to staunch wounds, to plug holes, to alleviate distress. The criticism is made that to concentrate on charity/love is to perpetuate situations of injustice. But this need not be so. Such is not the fundamental Christian or philosophical view of love or of benevolence. That view takes into its sweep all that is required for the full flourishing life of individual and community: it cannot be satisfied until that is achieved. Love is not love if it confines itself to almsgiving and ignores the great human needs of equality, freedom and justice. There is no clash between love and the struggle for liberation or for the change of structures. Rather one demands the other. Love must calculate how best to deal with every situation in the light of its thrust towards full life for all.

We have come to see that we must ask ourselves more seriously what are the needs of others and—especially in the case of the underprivileged and marginalised—what it is that prevents them from attaining even the minimum of decent living conditions. Perhaps that is only successfully done by those who are prepared to share their lot and listen to their agenda. It is clear that if love is to be realistic today it must be concerned to search out the causes of injustice, to listen to social analysis, to take politics seriously and to be ready for the abandonment of privilege at national and international level in favour of those who are oppressed by the structures which over time our world community has imposed on them.

Making Love Central

We have been thinking of morality in terms of love, taking the line that love is its central axis. One of the claims that is often made about the ethics of the New Testament—and certainly one of the general impressions that comes across—is that Jesus *did* centralise morality around love: love is the greatest commandment, the first; it appears to relativise everything else. One can discern in New Testament ethics a shift of perspective in which the person becomes central and other considerations about Sabbath regulations etc. assume a very secondary place. I said at the outset that one got the impression from the standard text books of morality that one

81

could be substantially moral while failing in love, but that in the last few decades an effort has been made to bring charity-love centre stage. What it means to say that love is central or primary is not entirely clear. But I take it to mean that all moral response is some expression of love. Our lives together are, of course, many-sided. Different aspects of them have their own appropriate moral response and their own virtue. Courage, temperance, fidelity to promises, justice, chastity are different aspects of morality. One does not want to take away from that. But they are all some version of the needs of living together in community and of the desire or call to live such a life in the way that respects persons and makes for their flourishing. In the end the justification of any moral rule is person-centred. One suggested way of putting this has been to say that all are mediations of love. Certainly, St Paul seems to have seen moral life in this fashion. For him love links everything together (Col. 3:14), other moral responses seem to be expressions of love (1 Cor. 13), indeed all the Commandments appear as the fulfilling of love (Rom. 13:8ff).

The effect of making love central is that morality is not seen as a jumble of disparate obligations or a set of unconnected rules. All morality is about concern for the welfare of persons in community. This does not mean that all is to dissolve in a vague blur or that it is not possible to have clear and definite moral positions, perhaps absolute positions. The thrust of what we have been saying is that one is to seek the true expression of love.

It is a pity that in recent times attempts to work out the rules of love have been denigrated by applying to them a dirty word—legalism. That was the thrust of the movement which in the sixties came to be known as Situation Ethics. Its central thesis was that Christian morality must be guided entirely by considerations of love. But some of its attractive catch-phrases implied an opposition between such love and moral rules. For example: 'Persons are more important even than standards'; 'The disciple is commanded to love people, not principles or laws'; 'For the situationist there are no rules, none at all'; 'Every little book and manual on "problems of conscience" is legalistic...This kind of intrinsicalist morass must be left behind as irrelevant, incompetent and immaterial'.[4] One should not allow a polarisation to be set up between love and legalism or between love of the person and moral rules. Those who try to work out the lines of true moral response are not ignoring persons: their effort is rather to protect persons. For instance, people ask why the Churches are interested in sexual morality. It is true that there may have been undue emphasis on this in the past, but anyone who is interested in persons must be interested in sexual relations precisely because there are few areas of human life with such possibilities for human happiness or suffering. Moral rules seek to save people from hurt.

On the other hand to make love central is to make great demands on moral teachers and authorities. In its purest form a morality of love says that an act is right if and because it is the loving thing, wrong if and because it is not loving: all moral principles are considered to be derived from and justified in terms of love. This means that wrong acts can be shown to be in the first instance a failure of love—and therefore wrong. This may not always be easy to demonstrate. Test it out for yourself on some of the well-known moral prohibitions. In the Irish divorce referendum of 1986 the central argument was about compassion or love, one side maintaining that to refuse divorce was to be lacking in love, the other that to grant it was a lack of love. How does one know or show what is loving? When someone asserts that certain kinds of act are unloving there may be a hidden agenda: there may be another moral theory (such as a natural law theory) lurking there. The key question to be asked here in order to check out a person's moral theory is: do you hold that something is unloving and therefore wrong; or do you hold that it is wrong (because contrary to natural law or some biblical precept, for example) and therefore unloving?

We must not underestimate the recasting of thought that may be involved here. Morality, we are saying, is not some unexplained set of rules imposed on us by God or by anybody else. It is rather the community's wisdom about successful living together. Anybody, of course, who undertakes to tell another or a whole people what is humanly good for them takes on a difficult task, is open to questioning about his/her position and cannot just toss off moral judgments without justifying them. One who presumes to make universal statements about what is good for anybody and everybody in all possible times and cultures—who proposes moral universals—is obviously taking on an even more difficult task. One of the questions which we must therefore confront later is whether in relation to love one can only give a once-off answer (i.e. this is what love means in *this* case), or whether one can successfully maintain that there are rules for loving (which imply solutions which apply to many cases), or even universal rules (which mean that this must be the way of love for everybody in all possible circumstances), or at least rules for not-loving (which say that nobody ever in any circumstances acting in this way can claim to be loving).

Love is to be the fundamental thrust of one's life. Virtues can be directed to various ends, good and bad. We admire courage, fortitude, perseverence, temperance, patience. But they may be used equally for selfish ends and too often they are prized without consideration of how they are integrated into life—the ambitious in business, politics, academic life or in the Church need all of them. A few years ago the Tory party took as its conference motto 'The Resolute Approach'. Resoluteness is a useful quality in pursuing good ends and in making such a pursuit one's way of life: it is important to moral life. But one can be resolute in pursuing selfish, inhuman objectives. The virtues find their true place in the service of love. Whatever other qualities one has there can be no genuine morality without an opening of the heart to others: heartlessness is incompatible with moral life.

Is there not a question here about how and why we pursue moral life? The whole enterprise might well be an ego trip, dictated by pride, by the need for security, or by a grasping for perfection/salvation. I think we have warnings enough in the Bible about that kind of attitude. Rather than see moral life as striving or grasping one might see it as surrender to the humanising and life-giving tendencies which we find within us. I have confidence that such do exist in us—that there is within us a deep strand of respect for others, an altruism towards them, even sometimes an extraordinary readiness to prefer their welfare to one's own. One can accept such as genuinely generous desires—and not necessarily as some deeply camouflaged selfishness. Christians in particular may be optimistic about this. They believe that the source and ground of life can be called Love. They believe that such love diffuses itself, that creation is an expression of love and that the salvific purposes of God in Christ lead to love and seek love: the good news of the kingdom leads to the morality of the Sermon on the Mount. They believe that the love of God is poured into our hearts by the Spirit who is given to us, that the dynamic of the Spirit is loving and that one who walks in the Spirit brings forth the works of love. They have in their holy books constant appeals to let the stories of the love of God and of Christ form their vision and character, to let the Spirit be their way of life. The totality of Christian moral life might be thought of as allowing the love of God to be abroad in the world through us, bringing about the reconciliation of all in Christ. To be open to others in this way—to care for their growth, to bind up their wounds, to try to humanise the structures in which they live—is to bring them some experience of salvation. It is also to reach one's own salvation—to find truly human life. It is—if we could only believe it—more blessed to give than to receive. It is in giving that we receive and in dying to self-centredness that we find life.

5

THEORIES: THE GREATEST GOOD: NATURAL LAW

CHRISTIAN judgment arises out of the vision of faith and out of character formed by the Christian story. Christians are to let the totality of the message bear on them and allow choices to emerge that are consistent with it. It is not a matter merely of observing a set number of directives. It is a call to an ideal which is uniquely realised in each one's circumstances according to each one's possibilities. St Paul and St Thomas Aquinas believed that the truly free do not need anyone to guide them in this task because they have their law inscribed in their hearts and are taught interiorly: they are led by the Spirit (Romans 8:2); the law is only for the lawless and ungodly (1 Tim. 1:8-9).[1]

This is a state to which we must aspire. But for most of us it remains more an aspiration than a reality. Paul and Thomas knew and acknowledged as well as we do that we need guidance because we do not allow ourselves to listen to the promptings of the love of God that is given into our hearts. We crowd out the Christian story. We do not listen to our true selves but let surface desires entice us. We confound the movements of selfishness with those of grace. We read the message as it suits us. We deceive ourselves—nowhere is it more easily done than in religious matters. We suppose that God is speaking to us, we rationalise, we cite Scripture for our purpose: it is one of the oldest temptations in the game; Jesus knew it in the desert ('It is written ... '). The high teaching of Paul and Thomas is for the free, the morally converted. So often in our lives we are not free.

We need guidance. Most of us, I think, however personal and unique our lives, do have at the back of our heads some checks and balances on choices, some kind of structure or scaffolding of morality within which we lead our lives. We do not—if we have any sense—go it alone. We accept from our tradition a set of moral beliefs or rules, mostly of a negative kind: do not kill, steal, lie, commit adultery, etc. We have more positively the general open-textured values of civilised society and the great thrusts of the Christian message (Chapter 3) which beckon us ever upwards to the heights. The rules with which we are confronted in society and Church mark rather the frontier of basic duty, the minimum conditions of stable community life. However lofty our Christian teaching, it is these rules that tend to dominate Christian life and they are often the flashpoint of controversy.

In this Chapter I am concerned more with these basic moral rules—but not in themselves. I am asking how we come to have them, how they are to be justified or grounded. It is good to be able to give an account of one's moral beliefs. If behaviour is said to be right or wrong there must be reasons for this. Can we get into the area of reasons: can we dialogue about moral positions? The more we can do so the better we understand ourselves, the better our contribution to society and Church, and the better we can serve those to whom we have a responsibility to hand on a moral tradition. It will not do any longer simply to assert—especially in matters of public interest—'Behaviour A is right', 'B is wrong', 'X is right', 'Y is wrong'. Why do we say so? Is it merely a matter of personal taste, of stubborness or of loyalty? If we are to have civilised discussion it is necessary to try to tease out and justify positions. To ask 'why', to try to give reasons, is to attempt to reach down into one's basic theory.

This is, of course, getting into deep water and you may have visions of balancing angels on the point of a needle. But debate about a fundamental moral theory or principle is one that has exercised the generations and is not likely to go away. And this is not surprising, because it is a debate about why one claims that anything is right or wrong. If you were to ask moralists generally or look at the history of moral theory you would find different views about that. You would get answers like: an act is right if it is the act which brings about the greatest good/or if it respects persons/or if it treats others as ends and not merely as means/or if it respects human rights/or if it respects the natural finality of a faculty/or if it pursues and defends the human good which intelligence proposes to us/or if it is in accordance with a principle which you would be willing to universalise/or if it is what people would agree to choose in some kind of contractual situation in which they would not know what position in society they would have/or if it provides for the basic needs of everybody concerned. Or, as we considered in the last chapter, if it is the loving thing to do. What a theory means is that someone is prepared to say something like the following: what I hold to be most fundamental about living is that one should treat others as ends and never as means and that is why I hold that to execute someone for a crime which he/she has not committed is wrong. The fact that people hold different moral theories does not mean that they will disagree about particular issues. They will frequently agree. But on some matters their different theories will lead them to different conclusions.

We cannot hope to solve this age-old question of moral theory. What I propose is to look at some theories which have been prominent in my tradition. In the first part of the chapter I look further at the implications of basing morality on agape-love. I then look at natural law theory. It has had its problems but it in turn has been sharply critical of the agape approach advocated by many Catholic theologians today.

A common definition of agape-love, as we saw in the last chapter, sees it as centrally concerned with seeking the welfare of others and of oneself. There remain great difficulties about this apparently simple principle and they bring in train serious issues about the relation of the individual and society. It is possible to interpret the principle as meaning that we are to love each one whom we encounter, that, as some put it, we are to live in covenant love with each one as God has committed himself to each. But surely this is limiting. Is my love to be confined to the people around me, those whom I meet? Is concern for the people I know to take precedence over those I do not know? Trying to love each idividual does not solve the problem. We have noted that we all live in a great number of intersecting circles. There are problems about who is to be loved or how many. All sorts of people are affected in different ways by a single act: moral problems are frequently about who is to benefit and who is to be left out.

Moreover there are wider issues of a social and political kind.

The people whom we wish to love are enmeshed in a great net of structures: we cannot love them without engaging the structures. We have touched on this already but need to look at it further. (We might again advert to the fact that there is an overlap between agape-love and other moral theories, that some moralists regard love as a version of such theories dressed up in biblical language, and that a morality of love sometimes borrows from or subsumes into itself other theories. In examining the implications of agape-love we will find ourselves touching on some of the major controversies in moral theory today. That is all to the good.)

IS MORALITY BASED ON DOING THE GREATEST GOOD?

I do not know what you would say if you were asked what moral theory lies beneath your judgments or beneath the moral rules to which you subscribe. Judgments even about one other have to balance good and harm: a surgeon may have to remove someone's arm or kidney. That is not so bad because you are seeking the welfare of just one person. But what do you do when there are several involved—perhaps the members of a family or community or State. You have three children. A move to a different town will improve the educational possibilities for two but one who is very happy with the teachers where you now live will suffer. How do you love them? How do you solve your problem? What kind of basic consideration comes into play. Many people, I think, would characterize their judgments in such circumstances by saying that they do the best they can or what is in the best interest of all concerned—what is best for the family, or community, or State. What does that involve? It seems that there is some kind of adding up of welfare and a choice of the alternative that brings about most welfare. How do you reconcile this with your care for the individual: if you judge that you should move in the case presented, how do you say you love the third child; is his/her welfare subordinated or sacrificed to the welfare of the others? It is difficult to know how to love several people together.

Many moralists—one could probably say most and in recent years an increasing number of Catholics—go along with this kind of thinking which adds up welfare. They regard it as the foundation of the common moral rules which we have. They state their moral theory by saying that of the alternatives open to a person he/she is to choose that alternative which will bring about the greatest good of those affected taken in sum or added up: that means the act which offers the greatest preponderance of good over harm. (We will call this the principle of the greatest good or the principle.) It is an attractive principle. One could see it as an excellent purpose for a Minister for Finance to have on budget day or indeed as an admirable foundation for a Government's whole social and economic policy. It is a very plausible interpretation of agape-love: if love means seeking the good of others the loving act would seem to be the one that brings about the greatest good.

The word 'good' is being used here in the now familiar sense of human or pre-moral good or welfare. We are not necessarily talking about the desires or wants of the people concerned but about their genuine good or well-being (and of course there may be difference of opinion about that). The supporters of the principle say that what is right action in any circumstances is discovered by weighing the effects or states of affairs which result from action. In calculating good and harm one is to count every person including oneself. Thus, in the example given above parents should also take into account their own good as well as that of others affected.

We are well accustomed to this balancing of different goods and to the balancing of good and harm. A teacher has to balance spending a lot of time on backward children with giving it to the brightest children in the class. Our society debates whether we should spend most of our educational resources on a small group of people at third level who may greatly benefit, or spread it thinly over the whole school-going population—whose overall situation would be slightly improved. We could spend our medical resources on high technology which would greatly benefit a minority of citizens suffering from, let's say, cardiac conditions: alternatively we could improve the general health marginally by spreading the money more evenly. What should a community do? A political party which is said to have a link with men of violence has been banned in Ireland from television screens under Section 31 of the Broadcasting Act. It would seem desirable, good for the country, that it—and people generally—have freedom to express its point of view. But perhaps this would give encouragement to violence. We sometimes ban books: the book 'The Joy of Sex' has been banned recently by the Censorship Board. There is no doubt that it would do some good for responsible couples: it might also do harm to the immature. What should one do? In the recent referendum on divorce we were told by our bishops to weigh the bad against the good effects of voting for the availability of divorce. Governments sometimes suppress important information 'in the public interest', as they say. And so it goes on. Many acts involve choices of alternatives: many have good and bad consequences. There does not seem to be any escape from the procedure of weighing and balancing.

The goods involved in this kind of judgment are of course very varied. So in the example above one would think of the physical, social and spiritual as well as the intellectual welfare, of the family concerned. We must add all the elements together and see what the sum comes to. Of course it might be very difficult to decide what act would bring about the greatest good. You have two children. One of them is very bright and the other is handicapped. The town in which you now live has a school for the handicapped but the bright one is not doing very well. A move to another town will greatly improve the opportunities for the bright one but the handicapped one would suffer. What would you do? How do you add up welfare in this case? Or do you add it at all? According to the principle, moral judgment is all about weighing consequences or states of affairs. Nothing is morally right or wrong in itself, it says, except to do or fail to do the act which brings about a preponderance of good over harm. So it is sometimes right to do acts that cause pain, loss, suffering, disappointment to some if they bring proportionately greater good to others.

But how far is one prepared to push this? Suppose a certain course of action would involve loss of life for one person but that others would greatly benefit from the action. Loss of life is indeed a very great harm but according to this theory there is nothing that cannot be measured—even loss of life or the killing of others—and until the final measuring is made one cannot tell what is right or wrong. We are to tell what is right and wrong in each situation simply by getting clear about the facts of that situation and then asking what act is likely to bring

91

about the most good. We are to apply this test directly and separately to each case with which we are confronted. (In love or agape terms you can call this 'act agapism'.)

Problems

What one is doing is looking to the effects or consequences of acts, to the states of affairs that an act or its alternative will bring about. But is doing the act that will bring about the greatest amount of good always the right thing to do? Is moral judgment solely about weighing consequences? Think of some examples. To kill the ruler of a country—I don't just mean a despot or tyrant but a poor ruler—might bring about good consequences. To drop a bomb on a Japanese city might hasten the end of a war and save more lives than would be lost in the city. To kill a foetus might bring much relief to a mother and contribute to her psychological health and to the welfare of her large family. Or it might save the life of a mother, or greatly relieve the distress of one who has been raped. To strangle a crying child who threatens to betray the movements of escapees might save them from certain death. To seduce a foreign diplomat might bring great profit to one's country and avert much harm.

Some more examples. There may well be pressure to sacrifice one person to the general welfare. The example is often given of the sheriff/judge of a town where a person has been killed, who is warned by a murderous gang that they will certainly kill five members of the black community if he does not execute someone for the crime: he frames an innocent man and defends his action by saying that in the end he saved four lives. The life of a great surgeon, artist, scientist or statesman/woman is in danger. One might prolong his/her life by taking a vital organ from some poor, unknown sick person in a ward of the same hospital. May one say that the undoubted advantage to be gained by the community justifies forcibly taking the necessary organ from this unfortunate? Could one think of doing it even if it were not necessary to kill the other but only to incapacitate him/her in some way? May one take the various organs of one sick (dying)) person if they would save two or three other gravely ill people? Is one justified in experimenting, let's say, on foetuses, as guinea-pigs in order to advance medical science to the benefit of the whole community? What kind of intervention—physical or psycho-logical—do you allow in the case of sex criminals in order to protect the community? It may well be that there are situations sometimes in which a community is in dire need and that the need can only be met by sacrificing somebody—we live constantly on the edge of such cases in the medical area. Would one be justified in experimenting on prisoners if it could give us a cure for AIDS? We can see how acutely the importance and value of the individual person arises in any theory that is centrally based on consequences.

Development of the Principle: Rules, Policies

Those who advocate the theory of seeking to do the greatest good know perfectly well that there are problems about it, that it seems to go against some of our moral instincts. But that does not disturb them. They point out that what we have been following is a very crude version of the theory and that if we looked more carefully at 'what is in the best interest of all concerned' we would find that killing the innocent—or ignoring promises or telling lies—are not the alternatives which bring about the greatest good. They suggest some of the following refinements.

First, it is important to think about the long-term effects of an act. Thus killing an innocent has very harmful effects in a community and while in some circumstances it may appear to give immediate improvement it would be very difficult to justify it in terms of long-term effects. The long-term (and perhaps even the short-term) effects on a community of knowing that any one of them could be taken out and killed if it proved expedient are almost incalculable. The second refinement to note is that institutions and conventions are important to a community. Thus, for example, it would cause bad consequences in a community if it were not a normal expectation that truth would be told, that debts would be paid, that promises would be kept, that contracts would be honoured. One would have to weigh very heavily the consequences of violation in these areas. A further refinement is the suggestion that the calculation which we make about consequences should not be about the effects of particular acts but about rules. What we should look for are the rules which would produce greater good and less harm if people regulated their conduct by them than if everybody followed a different set of rules. So keeping promises, paying debts, telling the truth, not stealing, not taking life are right acts not necessarily because in a *particular instance* they produce the most good but because greater good follows when everyone observes such rules. They are the best policy for a community. This development admits that there can be conflict of rules: in such a case the less weighty rule will yield to the more weighty. (In agape terms you could say that these rules are the way of love and you could call this version of the principle 'rule agapism'.)

Several Catholic moralists follow the general line of basing morality on a principle of bringing about a preponderance of good over harm. This is interesting because traditional Catholic moral theory did not arrive at judgments in this way. It regarded some acts as wrong by their very nature before and without any balancing of pre-moral good and harm. But now you find many subscribing to this theory, and that is partly the reason why there are differences between Catholic theologians on some crucial issues. You find them saying, for example, 'that we must determine the moral rightness or wrongness of an act by considering all goods and evils in an act and evaluating whether the evil or the good for human beings is prevalent in the act': the harm is justified, they say, in terms of the whole act by the proportionately greater good.[2] They stress the refinements just mentioned. They are careful also to insist that one must ask whether the gaining of good effects does not involve the undermining in some sense of the good that is being sought: if so the action makes no sense. Concern for human life—the very concern that is present in the desire to save four lives, for instance—is undermined by the deliberate killing of an innocent. (This group is sometimes referred to as Proportionalists. It is a useful term and I shall hold on to it.)

Do we Need other Principles?

I do not know at this point what you think about the principle as a general theory on which to base decisions, whether you are prepared to stick with it and whether you regard it as an adequate basis for the common moral rules. (I wonder how you solved the problem of the two children—one very bright, the other handicapped.) There are plenty of moralists who are prepared to stick with the principle as an entirely adequate foundation for morality. There are others, as we shall see, who reject it out of hand and who sharply criticise its adoption by Catholic moralists.

There are others still who adopt a middle position: they regard it as a large part of the foundation of morality but believe that it needs to be supplemented by other insights. They say that it cannot easily accommodate considerations which they regard as an essential part of our moral awareness. They make the point that the general theory of seeking the greatest overall good does not seem to be able to accommodate justice considerations easily. It says predominantly that one adds up the total good of an action without consideration of how the good might be distributed. It is the best total sum of good or welfare that matters. It does not in itself say that everyone should get a fair share of the benefits that a country can give. Nor does it make allowance for the worst off. It only says that we should do things and organise our society in the manner that will bring about the greatest overall good.

But how precisely is that to be interpreted? If altogether it would bring about more welfare to concentrate resources in the capital city (and on a simple calculation it probably would, since so many of the population live there), then that would appear to be the right thing to do, forgetting about the regions. Given a choice—let us say in a matter of economic policy or taxation—of making a thousand poor people somewhat better off or making two thousand middle class people considerably better off, the principle of doing the greatest good would seem to indicate a choice in favour of the middle class. But are we happy with that? The point that is being made is that fairness in distribution, concern not for the totality but for the individual and some kind of preference in favour of the worst off are part of our moral heritage and of our moral sense and that considerations of overall good do not seem to accommodate them. There are those who believe that the worst off and especially those on the breadline (and one can be on the breadline in several different senses) should be cared for first by any community, that there should be, to use the modern term, an option for the poor.

One can argue of course that the principle meets this, that judgment in favour, say, of the capital city or of the middle class or neglect of the poor would make for a lot of unhappiness

95

and would not be in the greatest overall interest. This is at least arguable but it is not sufficiently strong to satisfy: there are those who would want to build into the distribution of benefits insights about giving priority to the worst off and to situations of greatest urgency—even though there will be situations in which it will not be plausible to say that this makes for the greatest overall good. What they propose is some combination of theories, one based on summing good or welfare, the other not derived from that but independently based on the dignity and needs of the individual.

Such concerns seem to be even more justified when one thinks about issues involving human life. One may argue, as we saw, that it would not be in the interest of the greatest good to put someone to death for a crime which he/she has not committed. But are there any conceivable circumstances in which it would be for the greatest good? And if so, what then? Certainly there are some moralists who wish to say that such an act is simply wrong and that one should never even *think* of measuring an innocent individual's right to life against a calculation of good consequences.

You can see the problem and the anxiety. The basic issue is how to protect and care for the individual in this theory. In the case of the three children, did you sacrifice the welfare of one to that of the other two? That judgment may be the only reasonable one. But are there ever issues in which the welfare of an individual should not enter at all into the calculation—or certain respects in which this should not happen? There are those who want to say so, while holding that overall the principle of the greatest good must inform one's general perspective. They want to respect the life and integrity of the innocent individual at all costs. They want to provide first and independently for the most urgent need. It is this that will lead some to judge in favour of the handicapped child in the case given above. Again one may justify it by saying that this is what brings about the greatest overall good. But that is hardly plausible and certainly one can set up the case in such a way (in terms of the amount of good that would accrue to each in the different alternatives) in which it is clearly not plausible. And yet many will still justify an option in favour of the handicapped. So perhaps we need an approach to moral questions which will show the influence of a number of insights—the principle of the greatest good, a concern for individual rights and an option for cases of greatest need and urgency. The response of love may be one that delicately balances these different elements.

THE NATURAL LAW TRADITION

There are moralists—philosophers and theologians—who will have no truck at all with a central principle of doing the act or following the rule that is calculated to bring about the greatest good and who would equally reject a morality of agape couched in such terms. That means that for them the rightness or wrongness of an act derives from some other criterion. They may be natural law moralists—to take one example. There are right and wrong acts or rules of conduct, they say, but they are not arrived at by calculating welfare. However, they would insist that one cannot be said to love others except by observing such rules in their regard—rules about IVF, contraception, pre-marital sex etc. They are seen as the rules of love. But it is obvious that such rules/acts do not have their first rightness because of agape: they are right for some other reason.

Theories of this kind have played a prominent part in the Roman Catholic tradition. I want to look at some of them and at the running argument which they have conducted with all theories of a consequentialist or proportionalist kind. For them moral rightness/wrongness is not discovered by summing non-moral goods but attaches at least *prima facie* to a certain kind of act—judicial killing, untruths, adultery, pre-marital sex etc. Once you know that an action falls under this description or has this concomitant you can say that it is wrong: you don't need to take into account further consequences, circumstances or intentions.

Here it is not a matter, as it is for Proportionalists, of giving great weight to the harmful effect of telling, for example, a slanderous lie and deciding perhaps that on balance it would be wrong. No, some acts are simply wrong. It is not that consequences are never relevant to moral assessment. But Roman Catholicism holds that adultery is wrong no matter what the good consequences; that masturbation is wrong even if the intention is the excellent one of obtaining sperm for analysis; that contraception is wrong no matter what benefit it might bring to a couple; that divorce is wrong no matter what the advantage to the parties—when they both want it, are living in a hell together, have no children, would both be likely to be happy with another partner, and even when their action would receive no publicity and would not have any effect on the community; that abortion is wrong even in cases of rape or when it would save the life of a mother of a large family and even if mother and child would die if nothing is done (I refer to direct abortion); that telling an untruth is wrong however great the good it would do, e.g. to save one's country or however great the harm it would prevent, e.g. preventing the Gestapo from finding fugitives etc. How does it arrive at such positions?

The most celebrated theory in the Catholic tradition is the natural law theory. It is the source of its basic teaching, especially on most issues of sexual morality. It is important to look at it because objection to some of these particular positions is based not so much on the precise issue in itself as on the more general problem of the acceptability of the natural law theory on which they are based. At the same time it should be noted that to speak about natural law is really to speak about a complex of theories and concerns. Do not think about it as a *law* that was made and promulgated by someone (God) in anything like our sense of law-making. It is nearer the truth to say that 'natural law' is a way of talking about the fact that human beings have an awareness of the distinction between right and wrong and can work out the main lines of that distinction. The most basic concern of the theory is one that has served humanity well, that has been found to be inescapable for it. That is that there is a moral basis to life which can be established, not just for believers but for all men and women, by reflecting on what it means to be a human person and that this must be respected especially by positive law. This implies that there can be appeal to an order of morality from positive law, that there is a more fundamental claim than that of the binding force of State law—or any other law. It is a consideration that has been the hope of those ground under by oppressive regimes or faced with the claim that might is right. In this respect the tradition has served the human community well.

There is a broad basis to the theory. It is that what is morally right action is in some way indicated by what we are, by what one calls human nature—that particular form of life that we distinguish as human. The insight is that it is intelligent to act in a way that preserves our human being, and that of others, and that promotes its flourishing, and that acting in a way that impairs it is anarchic and meaningless. This consideration has arisen for us several times already in this book. Many people would, I think, agree with it as a general position. When we recognise then that a certain kind of activity is right and its opposite wrong what we are recognising is that it preserves and promotes our being as humans or fails to do so.

It is when one comes to spell out what activity is in accordance with our being that the problems arise. One finds that in the medieval tradition, borrowing from an earlier tradition, there were two main responses to that. One response stressed that right living (natural law) is 'what nature teaches all animals', the other that right living is what our reason tells us and that we find some pointers to that in the great inclinations or thrusts that are characteristic of human beings. In the first version moral living would seem to be discovered by following the lines of physical/biological nature with its faculties and their obvious purposes or ends, e.g. sexual faculties. These factual, physical orientations or 'laws' or purposes, this approach seems to say, indicate what is *morally* right. It is moral to act in a way which respects their 'natural power', 'process', 'purpose' or 'efficacy', immoral to frustrate it, to 'act against nature'.[3] In the second version these do not have a decisive voice: one is to use one's reason to discover how to live; the natural, physical orientations might well have to take their place in a broader judgment about what constitutes intelligent living. It was the first version that became dominant in the nineteenth and twentieth century manuals of theology and that was accepted into the official teaching of the Church.

Problems
The biological/physical version takes a very limited view of the human being and his/her flourishing. It reveals also, I believe, an outmoded way of thinking about God and his relationship to the world. The medieval way was to regard what is—nature—as the word, the design, the blueprint of God. Everything had its law determined by God—stones,

trees, beasts, and also human beings. The law of human beings was in their nature and that was found in the faculties-ends structure. That was how God made them. That was how they were to live. In this version biology reigns supreme: reason's only function, it seems is to note and accept the biological lines. But why should one order one's life by submission to the faculties-ends structure? Why should this be what is morally right? Can one be sure that this indicates how God wants us to live? It is this question which is at the heart of the debate about contraception—it serves as a useful illustration.

There are different elements of argument in official documents, but in the end it still seems to be the case that contraception is held to be wrong because it prevents the natural outcome of the act. (cf. *Casti Connubii* and *Humanae Vitae*, n. 16). But why, one asks, is that wrong? Is it wrong because it is an interference with the biological laws which God has put there? But why is interfering wrong? (Or if the argument is that it separates the unitive and procreative purposes why is that wrong and how does one distinguish 'natural' and 'artificial' means?) Statements about interfering with the natural outcome etc. are factual statements. But how does one move from that to a moral assessment? To say that contraception is wrong because it prevents the natural purpose of the act does not advance the argument unless one can show that preventing the natural purpose is morally wrong.

Such statements are sometimes reinforced by saying that God wants us to act in accordance with our biological laws. Does he? How do we know? Just because they are there? God has given us much else besides our physical and biological laws—in particular our intelligence and creativity. Culture—what we can do and make and bring about—is also a possibility from God—and not merely nature. The problem is to discover what it is that enables us to be human and become more human—what in our doing and making, what results of our creativity, are in accordance with intelligence and therefore with God's purposes for us. Certainly not everything and anything which we can do is right. But what? Why is anything right or wrong? Why are 'natural' means of birth control regarded as right and 'artificial' as wrong? (There are those who defend the distinction on other than 'natural purposes' grounds but the traditional position seems to run along such lines. The point can be made, however, that official teaching is not necessarily linked to argument and may not be greatly concerned to propose it.) What is our criterion?

Development: Values and Goods

The criterion must be a more adequate notion of human nature, one that encompasses the wholeness of the human being and is not limited to one element of it. The nature of a person includes a body but it not exhausted by it: it is crucial to take account of a person's whole existence in all its social, psychological, intellectual and religious dimensions. One does not discover what it means to be a human being by limiting nature to the physical. Obviously one needs a broader conception. It is not only that this will add something to the physical structure but that the physical structure will not of itself be allowed to be the determinant of what it means to act humanly.

This brings us back to look at the total human being and ask what kind of activity contributes to well-being or fulfils us—what are our goods, what is good for us? We have been in this territory before. We saw that there is a wide variety of such goods. We said that we know a lot about them and while at times our desires make confusing demands on us we can—at least in our better moments—recognise what is true fulfilment for ourselves and others. (There is nothing mysterious about this: we refer daily to inhuman or dehumanising conditions under which people have to live: we know what it is to be human.) This gives a much broader perspective on right living than concentrating on the physical element. What we are saying now is that right living (natural law) means acting in the way that is indicated by these goods, that promotes them for ourselves and for our whole society. This will take account of our physical make up but is not subordinated to it: what is good for it will be considered (e.g. the need for food) but it is only part of a much broader picture; judgment cannot be determined by it because human nature is not determined by it.

There is wide agreement about what fulfils, about such goods. But after that there is sharp division among Catholic moralists. We know what a Proportionalist would do now. He/she would say that one is to perform the act or follow the rule that brings about the preponderance of good among the various goods which may present themselves. But there has emerged in recent times a fairly well-defined school whose position is also based on a consideration of the great thrusts or aspirations of human beings and on the values and goods which they basically seek, but who diverge entirely from the Proportionalists on how human goods are to be sought and pursued.[4] They are very influential and many see their manner of argument as the best defence of traditional Catholic moral rules. They regard the idea of weighing diverse goods as completely impracticable. But that is not their fundamental objection. That concerns the very nature and structure of moral judgement. Theirs is a very complete statement of position so at the risk of some repetition of material let us follow the general lines of their argument. They start from the great human thrusts towards fulfilment—summarised as the tendency to preserve life, the tendency to mate and to raise children, the tendency to seek certain experiences which are enjoyed for their own sake, the tendency to develop skills and to exercise them in play and the fine arts, the tendency to explore and question, the tendency to seek out the company of others and to try to gain their approval, the tendency to establish good relationships with unknown higher powers and the tendency to use intelligent and guiding action.[5] This is the inbuilt programme of human fulfilment. These tendencies point to objects which we are to seek. Thus the end/goal/object of the tendency to explore and question is knowledge: we know that we should seek this and that it is good for us.

This school has made the matter precise by offering what they—with slight variations from one to the other—regard as an exhaustive list of human goods. Such a list is: life (including physical integrity, health and the handing on of life to others); knowledge of various forms of truth; play (engaging in performance which has no point beyond the performance); aesthetic experience; friendship (including various kinds of community and love); practical reasonableness (including self-determination, authenticity, integrity and the harmony of an inner peace of mind); religion. We know that to be human is to seek and respect such goods. Their pursuit and realisation occur in various ways but must always be in a way that totally respects the good in question. Thus the good of life is pursued

102

by famine relief, road safety laws, medical services and presumably by rescue attempts, laws about dangerous chemicals and drugs, food description acts etc: but not by suicide, killing of the innocent, transgression of another's bodily or mental integrity, contraception.

These are the true goods for us, they make for our basic well-being. But the authors are not interested in determining what is right action by comparing and weighing up these goods in any particular instance and opting for the act that brings about the greatest good. Quite the contrary. If what they have outlined are the genuine human tendencies and if the goods listed are the true human goods how, they ask, can one achieve one's own or another's good by acting against them, by choices that reject them? So their theory states that our fundamental responsibility is to respect each of those aspects in each person whose well-being we choose to affect, and that we never have sufficient reason to set aside that responsibility. It says, 'Respect every basic human good in every one of your acts'. Or 'Do not choose directly against any basic human good'. Desire for one good should never move one to choose to destroy, damage or impede another basic human good (whether that same good or another)—even in the most complex moral situations. Certain kinds of action are therefore wrong. So: no suicide, no killing of the innocent, no contraception—for human life is a fundamental value; no blasphemy—for a right relationship to God is a fundamental value; no injustice—for friendship in society is a fundamental value; no lying—for truth is a basic value and can be directly at stake in communication. And so on. Consideration of good consequences is not allowed to complicate the moral landscape. This school maintains that all the goods listed are equally important to being a human being. No one of them can ever be sacrificed to another. They cannot be weighed against one another. They are all equally fundamental.

COMMENT

The Basic Disagreement

This is a very rigid and unyielding position and runs entirely counter to what we have seen of the viewpoint of Proportionalists whose perspective is that in the complexity of human life it is not possible to pursue all goods independently. To promote or obtain one may involve acting against or sacrificing another. In that case what it is right to do is not discovered by respecting each good absolutely, not therefore from the kind of act in question. It is only discovered when one weighs the various goods that present themselves in particular instances and discovers which preponderates i.e. which is the most humanly serious and important. It is in this way that one makes a moral judgment.

Thus, they say, it is per se desirable that people be told the truth. It is also per se desirable that life be protected. But it may be necessary to go against truth sometimes in order to protect life. It is per se desirable that sexual intercourse be open to new life. It is also per se desirable that married people be able to express their love sexually and be able to have the number of children that does not impair health or living in harmony. The former may have to yield to latter. So that it is legitimate to act in a way that does not seek the former good.

The theory which we are now considering however says that desire for one good (for life or marital health and harmony in the examples just given) should never move one to choose to destroy or impede another basic human good (truth, openness to life). This gives it a system of moral truths or rules each of which is sacred: one may never go against any of them even where one appears to be faced with a clash of values.

How do you find this position? What do you think of it? There have been questions about it. The fundamental one is why one may not act against a good. The answer presumably is that it is irrational to do so. But this is not easily and immediately obvious. Is it part of rational insight that these goods are to be sought always and in every instance at whatever cost to the human being? Goods are goods because of their relation to and the way in which they serve the fulfilment of the human being: they do not have a life of their own. The other point of view is that in some instances respecting a good appears not to serve the whole person—because of the complexity of life situations—and that it is not unintelligent to act against a good (which is one sliver of human flourishing) when being bound by it makes impossible the total wholeness or welfare of the person. Who is injured when this is done? What is injured? The Proportionalist asks such questions and claims that when a particular line of action is needed for the welfare of a person it makes sense to choose the good that best serves this. He/she will ask not only why one may not act against a good but when one is acting against a good—knowing that some form of acting against a good must be allowed by all (as in indirect abortion, indirect killing, the use of 'natural' means of birth-control, etc.) and that this rigid theory depends to an extent on making a sharp distinction between direct and indirect intention. We will have something to say about that in a later chapter.

Humanisation

The fundamental thrust of natural law thinking is valid. The right way of living, of doing, is determined by the structure of the human person in community. In the most general terms the human good is what enables one to be fully a person—to be and to be fully: it is rational and intelligent to act towards self and others in the way that promotes that goal. We are talking therefore about activity that humanises: the person is central. There is no reason why natural law thinking cannot be cast in this form, and in this perspective it is a form of agape-morality. The problem which many have found with the version of natural law which dominated Roman Catholic morality was that the whole person was not kept in view: certain aspects seemed to be given a significance and prominence out of relation to the total person.

The ongoing task, of course, is to understand what it means to be a person, to discover what are the lines of human wholeness, what humanises, what are genuine human goods. We should all have views about that. But we should not expect to be able to prove that a piece of behaviour is inhuman and therefore immoral as clearly as we can prove something in the natural sciences. It is not something that can be easily 'read off' from a definition of human nature. It requires the experience of living and communicating as human beings. Moral 'proof' involves an appeal to one's sense of what it means to be a human person and some people have a more sensitive and developed appreciation of that than others. Every advance in the behavioural sciences should have something to say about it also. The physical/biological structure of the person is important, so are the social, psychological and religious dimensions. But, overall, the totality of the person must be kept in mind.

Not so long ago one of our national papers carried the heading: 'Bishops Say IVF Dehumanises'. They are right to think of morality in terms of humanising/dehumanising. But does it (in the so-called simple case) dehumanise? Can one say how and why it dehumanises?

Neither 'Natural' nor 'Law'

We should not use the term 'natural law' too glibly. It is produced often in moral argument like a rabbit from a hat—as if the very appeal to it clinched an argument. It does not. To say that something is a matter of natural law is to say roughly that its morality/immorality can be known by reason alone without recourse to religion or revelation, can be known by all people and is to be respected by all. It is to say that a moral position can be defended at the bar of reason. To make the claim about a particular issue is one thing, to show or demonstrate it is another. The term 'natural law' is at best the beginning of an argument, not the end. (It was thrown around carelessly in our recent referenda. I heard a politician claim on television that the form of wording in the 1983 abortion amendment was a matter of natural law: that was a claim of huge dimensions and he made no effort to justify it.) It would be wrong also to think that the expression meant to convey that truths of natural law are obvious. The idea that it is easy to know the details of the natural law or that most people can be expected to know them is foreign to the thinking of Aquinas.

Indeed one must have problems with both words—whatever the expression is meant to convey it could be said that it is neither 'natural' nor 'law'. 'Natural', 'natural tendencies', 'according to nature' are surrounded with difficulties. 'Natural' as opposed to 'artificial' is perhaps even more difficult—although some versions of natural law have depended greatly on it. It is not 'natural' either if that means that knowledge of morality comes easily or does not have to be worked at, teased out and justified. It is 'natural' perhaps only in the sense that the experience of morality is a general human experience.

'Law' too has its problems if it has the connotation of a rule or directive formulated and imposed by someone outside us: God does not impose the natural law on us in that sense. It is we who are the authors of the natural law: it is we who make or discover the law. God is the author of it in the sense that he is our author but he is no more and no less the author of the laws of morality (natural law) than he is of the laws of logic. It is obvious too from what we have said that the term 'natural law' has a history and that there are different versions of it—and perhaps it is true to say that it is the least creditable version that had the greatest influence on Roman Catholic morality. Those who try to elaborate an understanding of it based on a broad notion of the person and of what serves that come nearest to the truth.

We started out this chapter with the question about moral theory, about the quest for a fundamental criterion of what is right. One wonders if any one moral theory can bear that weight, if any one is adequate to the totality of our perceptions. Situations are complex and so is moral insight. It is not easy to measure or give priority to these insights. Morality arises out of the perception of the demands of being a human being with others in community. To say that it is centrally about love seems to me to be a reasonable position and one that can accommodate a natural law perspective. A general thrust and intention of seeking to bring about as much human good as possible seems morally admirable. So numbers are important—but not all important: the general principle needs to be supplemented by others. Rather than dominate the moral field it must stand with other insights which specifically safeguard the individual and form a bulwark against any easy subordination of the individual to the totality. It is not that one is setting the individual over against the community but that community flourishing, the welfare of all, is best under-stood not as a subordination of each to an impersonal sum of good but as a context which ensures that in certain crucial respects the uniqueness, sacredness and needs of each are respected.

In that regard the natural law tradition has been of outstanding importance to humankind. It has not been alone: some philosophical theories, especially those founded on human rights, have been allies. One must hope that renewed natural law thinking will press its points—the advance in tech-nology has greatly increased the threat to the individual. But it may be that it is from a sensitive combination of insights that the truth will be found. There is much agreement about basic well-being, about integral human fulfilment, between the different viewpoints which we have considered. They differ about how it is to be realised. However important the contribution of the natural law tradition it is not of its essence that it be a set of absolute (universal) rules—in the past it has made room for a comparison of values and for exceptions to rules. Whether and when that comparison and subordination should be made is the outstanding question.

Basic Morality

We approached this chapter as a search for a foundation for our basic morality. Perhaps this is an appropriate place to ask a question about that basic morality. I am interested here in the content of it, in the range of our traditional set of rules. They were elaborated in a different culture and social order. Perhaps we need to look at them. Not so much to change them—though we might need to change the emphasis—but to extend them. We tend to limit our morality in practice to the one to one situation and to a few well-worn issues. Right living—agape—now demands more sophistication from us. Irish Catholicism, I think one could say, finds it difficult to concern itself with the morality of politics and with social and community morality—to regard them as more than an optional interest or even to see them as issues of morality at all.

What we have been labouring through in this chapter is relevant. Every political, social and economic programme is some version of the relation of the individual and the whole community. It has implications for basic human well-being, for even the first outlines of the appearance of God's kingdom. It seems to me that moral concern—agape—demands that we show more interest in the theory—if any—which undergirds public policy: that is where our fellow human beings are either being treated with respect or oppressed—and we are responsible. The claim of a government to govern, its claim for example to withold part of one's wages in tax—an arrogant act in some respects—must ultimately be a moral one. It is—presumably—a claim that this is in the best interest of the community. How 'the best interest of the community' is understood and by what means it is to be pursued—by what combination of protection of the individual and his/her goods (autonomy, freedom, privacy, integrity, creativity) and care for the totality, by what reconciliation of maximum good and concern for the most deserving—is largely what this chapter has been about. (We have had no shortage recently of clear issues of this kind in the social, the economic and the political sectors.)

Perhaps this sounds dreadfully impersonal. But anything less does not take seriously the call of the other on us in a complex society amid contending claims and needs. Sensitive concern for each individual encountered will always be part of Christian life. But more and more, right living—agape—must concern itself with policies and structures: however great the inspiration of the agape-tradition it does not absolve us from the hard graft of finding the way of love. That demands reflection on how the basic well-being of all will be achieved, on the moral structure of society.

THE MORAL AGENT: UNDERSTANDING OURSELVES

OUR concern until now has been with what is morally right and in the last few chapters we have asked how we might proceed in discovering that. Such work is very important for a community—we shall have to return to it in the next chapter. To engage in it is to acknowledge that there are right (or at least wrong) answers to moral questions. It is to recognise that there is a truth for living, that there are real values for society. Moral theory is therefore important for a community. Moral positions have to be worked at, argued about, justified. All that, however, is at a very theoretical level and could give a false impression of what moral discernment and action are actually like. We must keep the theoretical level of discussion in mind but we need also to come down from the rarefied atmosphere where philosophers and theologians discuss in order to look at how in fact people (ourselves and others) make moral decisions and develop their lives, how they become moral persons or characters and what influence character has on discernment and action. Human beings are not machines or specimens of pure rationality. We can behave as if we thought they were, as if all that mattered for a community was to inform people about the right answers and have them do as they are told—as if their moral worth and their holiness could be judged by their response to that.

Moral insight and response are more complex—and I would say more interesting—that that. It is not sufficient that a community have the right answers. What an individual person will see, how he/she will respond, what he/she can do, how he/she will perform an action need to be looked at in a way that takes account of the flesh and blood reality. We need to look not only at what is to be done (which was the concern of the last few chapters) but at the human agent to whom this moral challenge is addressed. In this chapter I have gathered together some considerations which touch the mysterious area of human seeing and doing—that private interior world which has its own strange geography, hidden from the observer and largely hidden from the agent also. We will be looking at the different capacities of people to make moral judgments and to respond to moral considerations. We will reflect on the significance of the freedom with which they act for the quality of their moral lives. We will consider the importance not only of what is done but of the way in which it is done. We will have some thoughts on character, virtue and story. They are not separate but related aspects of our response to reality.

Moralists of an older generation did not have much to say formally about such matters. They assumed, I think, a high level of competence—competence both to understand morality and to act well—in the human agent. Church practice largely went along with this. It is true that the moralists tried to show appreciation of factors which affect freedom and imputability: they did the best they could with limited knowledge; their hearts were in the right place even if they did not have the courage to trust their instincts sufficiently. Pastoral practice too was often more benign than the text book: indeed one often met priests trying desperately to find a justification (and suffering pangs of conscience as a result) for a more understanding approach, one more in line with the capacity of the individual. Today happily we know more. We have learned something from the expertise of psychologists and moral educators. The problem now is to make connections: the concern of the Church is still predominantly about declaring the moral law, about objective morality. That is about an ideal world. There is not enough thought about what it is actually like for people to face moral issues, not enough about how people can become moral or indeed about what it means to act morally. And there is not much allowance in Church discipline for people's limited ability to understand and respond to moral reasons—one has only to note the summary dismissal in official circles of brave efforts to make room for a concept of gradualism in moral life. By gradualism I mean that at any point in our lives we are all capable of only so much, and can at best only take small steps. We must give more attention to the individual and to his/her capacity for morality.

Let us look then at the capacity of people to make moral judgments. The tradition, I think, assumed that all—apart from severely disturbed categories—could appreciate the moral demand when it was presented to them and could respond to it if they had goodwill. We have come to realise that in fact people may not be capable of appreciating such demands: what some acknowledge as an obvious and compelling moral call may not seem at all necessary or compelling to others. We know now that all of us pass through stages of moral development. We know this best, I suppose, about children and some will have had the experience of proposing to children a morality that is beyond their ken. You may have appealed, perhaps, for forgiveness and forebearance in a squabble among children to be met with the firm reply 'It is not fair'. What you were proposing simply did not appear right to the child. It is hardly surprising that specialists in the area of moral development differ about its stages and about the relation between the cognitive and affective aspects. What is agreed is that there *are* stages and—to put it generally—that appreciation of morality is something that matures only gradually. So that there are different forms of moral judgment: indeed the term 'morality' can only be analogously applied to the different stages. We know now that there is not much point in putting considerations to a child that are beyond his/her stage: what a child sees is what he/she sees: this is his/her understanding or grasp of what living with others means.

It is important to remember that this does not apply only to children. Adults too will have only more or less successfully negotiated these stages: we are all stuck somewhere between a childish 'morality' and a morality of principle. About this I have in mind two distinguishable but related aspects of human response: (*a*) the extent to which we are able to recognise moral claims or considerations (the judgments of which we are capable): (*b*) our ability to respond in free, deliberate action (the quality of our action, its humanness). I take it to be the case about human activity that there is a possibility of movement upwards from the blind instinctual activity of the child in response to need—the activity of getting what serves the need—to something that is at the further end of the scale

112

i.e. virtuous action arising out of responsible and interior appreciation of the good. We catch different aspects of this last state when we describe it as a movement to awareness, consciousness, presence to self, self-actuation, interiority, freedom. I assume that the ideal of human and Christian life is a pattern that exhibits these qualities in openness to true values. How that state and style of life can be realised or facilitated—by what happy combination of training and trusting, of effort and gift, of movement and waiting—is a question for the sages. Some of us may hardly get started on the journey—we not infrequently hear it said of an adult that 'he/she is still a child'. Those who do get started blunder into the snares that all who have gone before us have had to discover too—an idealism that forgets the body, a trust in naked will-power that is out of harmony with desires, a lethargic surrender to fatalism. What concerns us here is that we are all somewhere along the spectrum between the child and the autonomous, integrated adult and that it has implications for moral life.

We need to be careful then about what we expect people to see or to be able to do. We need to be careful about praise and blame. We have to take the individual seriously and his/her grasp or understanding may be a long way from the method or procedure of a philosophical or theological treatise or from the perspective of a Roman document. It is not a matter of bad will. It is that one cannot enter into that (more complete, superior) mode of perception, of knowing. Neither is it mainly a matter of intelligence. Moral insight is blocked not only by lack of clarity about the facts and an inability to argue consistently but by inadequate personality. How responsible we are for that is a moot point—not very, perhaps. So much goes into the making of personality—our genetic code, the influence of parents, early learning experiences, race and sex, culture and environment, the values and expectations of those around us. They have shaped our elemental urges and overall we have laid down a pattern of perception, desire and response before we have come to—or come far towards—consciousness. They are, if you like, the givens of life. Fate. The fact is that at all these levels and in all of these distinct elements fate has been cruel or kind to us.

Some have been lucky. They have lived in a bright and airy

land where moral considerations are a subject of everyday conversation. They have experienced warm, supportive and accepting structures—the old people, in John Montague's lovely image, like dolmens around their childhood. They have come to know what love, trust, respect and friendship are. They have noticed the satisfaction which those around them get from honest effort. Perhaps they have seen people ready to sacrifice themselves for high ideals. Somehow they have been prepared for moral life—at least they have a good chance. Patterns of receptivity have been laid down, desires have been fostered, affections have found direction.

Others have had cruel luck. They have been born into structures that crush their sense of significance and self-esteem. They have known no kindness. They have lived in suspicion. They have learned not to trust life or others or the future. They have known only tawdry pleasure. They have no sense of participation, no stake in things, no sense of identity. They see no point in looking upwards. They are as handicapped in respect of moral possibilities as one who has lost his/her sight is handicapped physically. It is not a matter of wealth or status—although the vast desolation of our cities seems to contribute to a slum of innermost being. Indeed it is often among the materially less favoured that one finds a climate of kindliness, trust and care—the Sermon on the Mount seems to say as much. While those who are born with silver spoons in their mouths may know only self-centredness or the arrogance that cannot bear to share, to be crossed, to be second, to fail.

FREEDOM TO SEE

These are extremes. But most of us have known a mixture of luck. The point is that we come to moral life predisposed or conditioned in certain directions. How we will see the moral call and what we will see of it is a function of our personality. Some may be so remarkably deprived that they can hardly be said to inhabit the world of morality at all. Moral considerations make no impact. They do not ring true or compelling. They exercise no fascination. They do not enter into one's purpose or outlook. Well-meaning people can explain or instruct or shout. It makes no impact. But we all suffer some astigmatism. With all of us there is some blurring of vision.

Moral judgment is a particular kind of judgment. It is a judgment about something to be done (and so we say a judgment of practical intellect). It engages our personality in a way that speculative judgment does not. Our inherited or developed beliefs and prejudices obviously enter into it but I want to look especially at the impact of emotion on it. Since it is a judgment about action on our part it is likely to involve us in what will be pleasant or unpleasant. That is why we have problems. Because it is here that the vast underground life of feelings and emotions operates—fear, anxiety, hurt, envy, anger, hatred, revenge, desire, delight, joy, longing. What touches us there touches us deeply and very much affects what we appraise as worth pursuing. It might be revenge (because I feel hurt or slighted, because someone has dented my self-esteem), vandalism (because I feel that I do not count, that life has dealt me an unfair hand), love, affection, sex (because I feel lonely, separate, afraid and want to be-with). We spontaneously tend to value and approve what feeds our emotional state and to flee what is painful to it. It is not just physical pain that matters to us but the more aching pain of feeling left out or not loved or not significant or not noticed or whatever. So judgment is dangerously liable to be clouded by emotional need. The result is that our perceptions are distorted.

Each of us has his/her own personal shape or configuration of this and each one's history determines just how emotions operate in life, just what intensity they have, just how they affect our perceptions. We looked at this before in Chapter 4 where we said that life is about conflicting desires: what we are seeing here is that the conflict is instigated by our emotions. Most people can also listen to a deeper level of desire, to the call of the genuine and true good. They can judge when it is appropriate to follow and integrate emotional desires. They are not swamped by them—at least not always. We said that life could be regarded as a problem of the education of desires, as coming to want the truly good as a pattern of life. That kind of conversion is a consummation devoutly to be wished. But most of our lives are much more patchy. Some lives perhaps are completely dominated by emotions—of rage, rebellion, sexual desire, hurt, hopelessness, ambition for power. But emotions drive all of us. We say of people that they are—at times or even as a general pattern—angry, anxious, happy, optimistic, dependent, cautious, spontaneous, scrupulous, that they are easily upset, hurt, excited, made fearful or enthused. We imply that they will tend to sense something harmful or frightening or threatening or exciting in a situation where others might not sense it. That will affect how they read and interpret situations, *what they will see.*

> They said, you have a blue guitar
> You do not play things as they are.
> The man replied,
> Things as they are
> Are changed upon the blue guitar.
>
> (Wallace Stevens,
> *The Man with the Blue Guitar*)

Feelings tend to distort reason at successive stages of the judging process—in marshalling and censoring facts, in understanding situations, in deciding what is to be done—the steps in which the moralist is crucially interested. The process of judgment is constantly in danger of being swamped and supplanted by emotions. If we were clearly aware of their operation things might not be so bad. But we are often blissfully unaware: they are in large measure subconscious—and therefore more powerful because unrecognised. It is not surprising to find people taking courses or seeking therapy so as to find out—beyond the brute facts that they are aware of—who they are and how they function, so as to bring the operation and influence of their emotions into the light. They may not do so from moral considerations but what they do has implications for their morality.

We are talking in a sense about the freedom of our lives but in an expanded sense of freedom. We usually think in terms of freedom to act. But behind and before that there is what might be called our freedom to see and judge. We are only half-free or half-willing seekers of truth: the factors which modify our freedom of action modify first our freedom of perceiving. We have great difficulty in seeing things as they are and not as we would like them to be. We have a problem with objectivity. The likelihood of our reaching it depends on our subjectivity, i.e. on the extent to which we can deal with the factors—largely emotional—which cloud our reading of situations. Test it out yourself in group discussions. Are you really open to discover the truth in the views expressed by others? Or do your dispositions towards them—your likes and dislikes—affect how you weigh what they say?

Truth, of course, exercises its own attraction. Goodness has its own emotional pull. We receive intimations of a higher life of truth and self-forgetfulness in all sorts of curious ways—perhaps on seeing a good deed, watching a play, hearing a story, or just having our hearts lifted by the first crocuses. Our imagination seduces us to goodness as well as to evil: that, I suppose, is at the heart of the natural law theory that we both recognise what is good and experience within us the desire to pursue it. Nevertheless to break through to truth or rationality is a considerable achievement. To be able to see what is the moral call in a situation requires a self-transcendence, a going beyond the immediate interests, likes and fears which often reside in our emotions. Few people have written better—or more depressingly—about this than Iris Murdoch. She says that the chief problem in morality is *seeing*: that our consoling wishes and dreams 'prevent us from seeing what is there outside us'; that our minds continually fabricate an anxious, self-preoccupied veil which partially conceals the world; that we cannot keep our attention fixed on the real situation or prevent it from returning to the self 'with consolations of self-pity, resentment, fantasy, despair'.[1] It is a gloomy picture—and it raises questions about one's view of human nature and human energies—but I think we all recognise some truth there. It would be a mistake to think only in terms of particular judgments and choices. Our point throughout has been that we do not really come afresh to each decision. We will see and judge as we are. It is not precisely the moment of choice that is the decisive one but all the moments that have gone into making it likely that this is how we would see and choose.

FREEDOM TO DO

So far we have been thinking about perception, about seeing. But there is the further freedom of action. The old moral manuals distinguished between the act of a person (*actus hominis*) and a human act (*actus humanus*). They were making the point that an action is attributable only to the extent that it freely proceeds from the subject as his/her choice. The fact that someone does an act does not mean that it proceeds from him/her in this sense. There are all sorts of depths in our acts. ('Depth' is of course a metaphor: we are dealing with the strange area of the sources of human choice; it is difficult territory.) An action can be more or less mine—and that goes for both right and wrong acts. We are long familiar with taking account of the influence of force and fear, as well as of other factors, on wrong action. We consider that they lessen imputability (responsibility) because there is a recognition that the action did not freely proceed from the person: it did not really represent his/her choice.

It must be equally true that right action is of moral worth only to the extent that it issues as one's real personal choice. What we want to know about a person is not so much what he/she did but the significance or meaning of the action. We want to know this in everyday life: the mere fact of giving someone a box of chocolates or a bunch of roses may mean much or little. It is important to note then that common moral concepts such as 'telling the truth', 'keeping a promise', 'being kind', etc. involve more than just a set of noises or physical movements. They involve the notions of intention, of understanding, of knowing what you are doing, of being free. It is possible to get people to go through or refrain from certain actions that look like cases of acting morally—either by inducing fear or by pandering to some morally irrelevant desire. But the value of this as moral action is doubtful and its final significance for the Christian must also be doubtful.

You could say that there is a whole spectrum of more or less moral activity. If there is a man at my door in need of bread I can train my dog to take bread to him. I may also be able to move a human being to a similar sort of activity—someone who is afraid of me or seeking to impress me or wanting to win my favour. It is true that the man gets his bread—good can be done and harm averted for all sorts of discreditable motives. But I am interested not only in the man who gets the bread but in the one who gives it. The action may not have produced any notable difference in the moral conduct of that person. His/her choice may not have been really a moral response to the other, not the kind of action that will make him/her good. At the other end of the spectrum is the totally free, mature, virtuous individual—rare perhaps—acting from inner conviction. The rest of us are somewhere in between. At least we ought to note the direction in which we should be moving.

What we have come to realise, I suppose, is that we need to expand the notions of pressure and unfreedom. There are not only external and palpable pressures but many internal pressures—the buried patterns of our emotional lives. Our feelings explain much of how we relate to society. They are often the clue to why we acted and even—as we shall see—to what we did. Feelings are not necessarily connected with action: we may just sit there and brood as we experience hatred and resentment. But feelings can be the powerful motive for action. It is a commonplace that when we look for the explanation, say of a murder, we look to hatred, jealousy, desire. They tell us why the act was performed. Likewise it can be said that our feelings and emotions 'get us' to perform what look like good acts when in fact they arise not from any response to genuine value but from the urgings of some less admirable emotions. We know how human respect, the emotional inability to say 'no', the fear of being thought a fool, the fear of what others will say, not to mention the influence of more obvious—even religious—fears can get us to perform acts that impress but that have only the shell of goodness. Even people in the caring professions are aware that their caring may be more a response to their own emotional needs than a genuine respect for others. A fair amount of this is below the daylight of reason in the subterranean caverns of our lives. It can be got at but only with difficulty.

So we are stuck with ourselves, with our personalities—do not forget that we have taken on good habits, desires and affections as well as more doubtful ones—and it is hard to know how answerable we are for them. However, the moral problem remains for each of us. It is what we are going to do with our lives at this point. The quite unique moral task of each is to respond now out of his/her particular history to the reality as he/she apprehends it. Quite unique, opaque, highly personal, embedded in each one's history. We are both limited and enabled by our personalities in a thousand and one ways.

But we are not simply victims of our history, not just objects tossed about by life but subjects who can respond to it. We have room to manoeuvre. Knowing my character you may feel that you can predict how I will act. Knowing that there are pressures on me you may well guess whether I will buckle under them or not. That does not mean that I do not have freedom—just how much is what is hidden from us. How free is one to change old ways of thought, to see things differently, to shed the inherited prejudices of class, creed, or race, to act against life-long (perhaps also inherited) resentment and bitterness, to ignore in practice deep hurts, to face down fears inherited from childhood, to give up alcoholism, to abandon a lifetime of debauchery, to leave a spouse and family with whom one has been living unlawfully for years? It is impossible to say in a particular case—note too that there are different kinds and nuances of unfreedom involved here. We just do not know. Nor do we have much of an idea, I think, of how the necessary conversion could be brought about.

People ask about freedom mostly in the context of praise and blame. There is a more positive aspect to the matter as we shall see. But praise and blame are important. Our obsession with them is usually religious: by that I mean that we are not so much concerned with the human moral quality of our actions as with their eternal consequences: was it, was it not a sin, etc? There is a further this-wordly angle to blame. That is the matter of Church discipline and it is here that institutions are rather helpless. An institution as large as the Church can only deal crudely with people—all divorces are treated as the same, all cohabitation, all falling from grace. It is important not to confuse a person's moral life or his/her condition before God with Church discipline: Churches cannot make morality or make sin. How they deal with a person may not correspond to the person's moral state. Mostly we do not have to judge our own freedom or that of others—fortunately. We can leave that to God. Those who think it is their business to judge ought to tread warily, for example priests in confession and those who administer Church discipline. They cannot see into that secret place which is the source of a person's fredom and of his/her acts. They cannot judge. Earlier Church practice was altogether too glib in deciding that people were in mortal sin. Happily in recent years many priests have come to realise that this kind of judgment is neither their obligation nor their right. It is useful to remember that the text books of moral theology which did their best with factors which diminish responsibility were written before modern psychology threw some light on the still obscure subject of human choice.

The more positive consideration is not about blame or punishment but about becoming human. True morality rests on true humanity. It must be an ideal for all of us to reach true freedom, to make our lives authentic and autonomous, to arrive at the point where choices and acts are genuinely our own, emanating from ourselves, a free response to true values. The glory of God is the person fully alive—humanly, morally. To reach this is a kind of liberation or salvation. It involves knowing oneself, being aware as far as possible of the springs of one's actions, being in possession of oneself and one's choices. That is slow and difficult work and there are implications here for moral education—indeed for any education—and for Church discipline. The emphasis must be on facilitating the growth to autonomy and responsibility and on lighting up the attractiveness of the values that lie behind the rules—so that people can appropriate them and act out of them. A form of moral teaching or of Church discipline that did not appreciate the significance of inner freedom, of autonomy and responsibility—that did not indeed encourage them—would be a disservice to morality and Christianity.

Thomas Aquinas had interesting things to say in this area: 'A person is said to be free if he/she acts from him/herself...because from virtuous habit he/she is inclined to do those things which the divine law demands'. And even more interestingly: 'He/she therefore who avoids evil not because it is evil but because of the command of God is not free but he who avoids evil because it is evil is free'.[2] Aristotle had said that a person is not brave who is forced to act bravely: bravery should be inspired by its own nobility; that presumably involves some appropriation of values. The doer, he says is just and temperate not because he/she does just and temperate things but when he/she does them in the way of just and temperate persons. So both Aquinas and Aristotle are saying that there is a close link between freedom and quality of moral action, between freedom and virtue. They are saying that the why and the wherefore of the doing are decisive and that factors which affect freedom affect this. They are directing attention away from the external act and trying to get at something more inward—as we have been doing in this chapter. They are pointing away from sheer doing to virtuous doing. That will include the intention in doing, the reason or motive, the disposition out of which and the desire with which one acts, even the facility with which one acts—in the deepest sense the freedom of action.

THE SIGNIFICANCE OF MOTIVE

Let us pursue this a little further. I want to look more closely at the notion of motive: it throws further light on action.[3] Moral action is a very complex matter: it is, as we have been saying, not just a matter of doing things. When we ask *what* a person did it is possible to give several different answers. A crude answer will just recount the brute fact. An answer from the moral point of view will have to take account of intentions, motives, dispositions, traits. Indeed the most appropriate answer to 'what?' is often found by asking 'why?' Take the act of giving alms to the poor. Can one discover what happened by concentrating on the external act? What looks like an act of giving alms may just as easily have been an act of self-aggrandisement, or of obedience, or one of seeking acclaim, or even one of humiliation of another. So we see that the motive for which a person performs an act becomes very important. For an act to be morally good it is a necessary condition that the agent to some extent recognise and seek it as such. This obviously raises questions about what is to count as moral activity and what we are trying to do in our moral teaching. It raises in another form also the problem of subconscious motivation and of trying to deliver people from pseudo-morality.

It is well then to look at that pair of words: 'right' and 'good'. We throw them around carelessly but they are meant to indicate an important distinction. Considerations of the right concentrate on the piece of external behaviour that is appropriate or justified. Almost all the debate among moralists has been about that. For example: may this attacker be resisted to death/may one steal in this case/is such an untruth justified in these circumstances/are there circumstances in which one may commit suicide? But even where resistance is justified one

122

may engage in it out of hatred. Even where a particular cause is just, one may engage in it out of vainglory or in order to gain votes or simply because it provides one with a suitable job. Even where a particular piece of behaviour is justified it may be done for a great variety of reasons. The action may be right but is it good? The last temptation of all, we say, is to do the right deed for the wrong reason. A morality couched in terms of precept/command/law emphasises right. So does a morality closely related to discipline/punishment.

The notion of 'good' gets nearer to the personal choice which in the end is the crucial element in morality. Whether an act is good or not depends on intention, motive, etc. There may be several motives involved and we have seen something of the insidiousness of subconscious motivation. (In a sense it is only the good act that in the end is the right act but it is useful to retain the traditional distinction.) Ideally one should act for the motive that corresponds to what makes the action right. That means that one should act out of love/respect/care for the other. Or out of some facet of that—for love of justice or truth or fairness. These are obviously moral motives: they are motives that arise out of moral considerations or from the moral point of view. The great issue for the community is to get people to be like this—to be the kind of people who can and will perform acts of this kind and quality—freely, consciously.

There are lots of motives that fall short of this. They may operate consciously or unconsciously. We may be well aware that we are doing the right deed for the wrong reason. The more disturbing fact is that there may be a whole tissue of motives, the residue of childhood anxieties and fears—to please, to be loved, to be the good boy/girl, to be safe, to be clean, to be sure and secure—that are the real springs of our actions and that are hidden from us. Our interior life is a fascinating country: what goes on there is far more interesting, complex and obscure than any novelist has thought up.

Religious morality presents a particular problem about motive. One may do a right act for the glory of God or for the love of Jesus Christ or for the furtherance of the kingdom. Christians often say that they love others for God's sake or that they see Christ in others. These are more properly religious than moral motives: Christians have both. We have seen in Chapter 2 that such religious motives are necessary to

123

the total Christian perspective and that they are greatly supportive of the whole institution of morality. It seems to me however that there is some lack here if the core moral motive is not present i.e. true respect or love for the other. If the glory of God is the human being fully alive that means the human being realising the moral dimension of life. However admirable our religious motivation it cannot absolve us from seeking that.

There are other religious motives which have played a notable part in our tradition and about which one is less happy. The appeal, for example, to fear and punishment may produce some kind of conformity and may prevent certain excesses—and the prevention of harm to ourselves and others is always to be welcomed. But such motives do little or nothing for morality. They do not make the person good. There remains the much more delicate job of educating the affections, of harmonising them with the good. Those who can touch others here are helping them to be truly and fully Christian. There may have been a problem in this respect with Catholic morality in the past. Is there a suspicion that the huge emphasis on reward and punishment diminished real moral concern, that there was some lack of humanness, that it did not genuinely take into itself real concern for virtue?

THE HISTORICAL CHARACTER OF LIFE: BECOMING

We can think about moral progress therefore as growth in a two-fold freedom—as freedom to be able to see the truth and to be able to respond to it out of personal conviction. In the course of life a person makes him/herself the kind of person who is more and more able to know and to do—or the opposite. Both elements represent an achievement and take time. In fact it is only the good person who will see clearly enough to make right decisions, i.e. in the first place only the one who wants to see, who has achieved some kind of openness. There is a very subtle relationship, therefore, between doing and seeing: Jesus told some of his hearers that it was because of the hardness of their hearts they did not recognise him. It is only the person who has faithfully done the truth in the past who will have the courage to look honestly now. Where there is such honest willingness one's antennae become more sensitive so that one gradually becomes more aware of what it means to live morally. Past victories are consolidated and one is ready for even greater generosity in the future. But the opposite can also be true. One can arrive at the point of not being able to see, of not wanting to see, of not being able to want to see. The moral point of view then makes no impact.

There is, then, a close relationship of past, present and future. The past has created the present base of operations and it is this that determines what will be possible in the future—what will be seen of the moral call and what will be the effective freedom of the subject to answer it. One is creating one's own possibilities or limitations. It is this kind of self-assembling project that is the moral life.

Many of us think of the individual predominantly as a doer of a considerable number of good or bad acts for which he/she will be judged. That is to think of moral agency in a way that is static and atomised. Moral life is more subtle and complex. People change not only the scene around them but change themselves by their acts. Acts remain with us in a sense, they embed themselves in our characters, we have to live with them forever. This is a point to remember particularly in a tradition that might suggest that we can simply get rid of our acts by going to confession. We cannot. For better or for worse we make ourselves particular kinds of persons. We bring a unity, control or consistency into our desires and traits. We become characters—with a certain moral shape, sensitivity and capacity so that we are moved or remain unmoved by considerations of a moral kind. It is nearer the truth to think of moral life not as a multitude of acts but as a project—that of becoming a person—an inescapable project into which each new-born babe is thrown. Not a project which comes cleanly to us either but one which has to be realised in the tangled circumstances of our psyche and our environment.

> This is a difficult land. Here things miscarry
> Whether we care, or do not care enough
> This is a difficult country, and our home.
> (Edwin Muir, *The Difficult Land*)

So, however freely or unfreely, one establishes a pattern of life. Some call it a basic or fundamental option. This does not mean that a person determines him/herself in one moment of intense choice. One cannot dispose of oneself in that way, cannot 'fix' oneself in a single decision: we all know that we decide something today and do the opposite tomorrow. But we do, over time, reach some kind of basic stance. Our life-span then is not so much a time for changing our minds as for making up our minds, deciding who and what we want to be. We sometimes find ourselves asking 'Who am I', 'What am I like'? It is an odd question but it is an attempt to reach below the individual acts so as to discover what the seminal or nuclear 'I' is like, to discover where we have set our hearts. We are not trying to discover some ghostly 'I'—'the ghost in the machine'. We are asking how we have integrated and directed our energies, how deeply we have been grasped by goodness or badness, how fully we have chosen them—and, as we have seen, that is not just a matter of what we have done but of how and why. It is this totality of character that determines what we can see, how what we see impresses or attracts us, what our possibilities are of responding to what we see and just how (with what motive) we will respond. You propose to two people the plight of some poor beggar or of those who are dying of hunger in Ethiopia. One will respond and do something about it and the other will not. Why? The facts of the case are for one a compelling reason, a motive for acting. For the other they are not. Why that should be so, why showing one person moral reasons is giving him/her a reason for acting (a motive) depends on the person's desires, on character.

In this connection it is interesting to recall that the Scriptures refer to the heart of a person which only God can search: we do not ourselves know what we are really like—we can only have presumptions. The Scriptures also distinguish sin and sins: the former refers to the state (the fundamental option) of a person of which the latter (individual acts) are only an indication. Because that option has become an engrained pattern in our desires it is not easy suddenly to be converted: there have been remarkable instances (or what seem like them) but they are, I think, unusual; changing one's heart is a difficult business and appearances can be deceptive.

To be realistic then, not only about what is theoretically right but about what is humanly possible, we need an understanding of the quite varying factors that have created this present person and his/her effective freedom: 'All the experiences were lined up waiting for me. I was born and there they were to form me, which is why I tell you more of them than of myself' (Saul Bellow, *The Adventures of Augie March*). We need a sensitivity to character—to an individual's beliefs, prejudices, affections, dispositions, weaknesses and strengths. We have been saying that life is a time for making oneself and that we must answer for what we choose. Yes and no. We do make ourselves but one has to be tentative in judging the extent to which we were free in doing so. We never escape from our past and much of it was not of our choosing: it is the past that has made the present and that modifies the future. My story is always the story of how I became who I am.

There is no use therefore in treating people as if at any moment they had absolute freedom to do anything that is put to them—to do the theoretically right. It is not just a matter of cranking up a naked will-power that is unrelated to who and where people are. What they can do, what can be expected of them, what God asks, what is a good and salvific moral response from them, depends on their circumstances. To reach truth and freedom is, of course, an important ideal for the individual, the community and the kingdom: there is no point in adding to the irrationality and confusion of situations, further compounding the 'sin of the world'. But there are different kinds of truth. In the inner recesses of each one's spirit is his/her mysterious personal response to truth and goodness. It is impossible to judge its goodness-value or salvation-value. If there are intimations of a better way and movement to conversion it will have to be by small beginnings, by starting back the road one has come. It is this realisation of the historical nature of human life that is behind suggestions that gradualism should be an accepted part of Church life and discipline.

STORY

We are our stories: it is the total story that can be told about us (the novel of each one's life) that explains who we are and why we are how we are and that gives a clue to what we are likely to do and to become. We also have our stories. One of our hopes must be that the remembrance of our Christian stories and especially their community recital in liturgy will have some

127

effect on the shaping of character. They can teach us morality, i.e. they can awaken moral sensibility in us, entice us into appreciation and desiring 'whatever is true, whatever is honourable, whatever is just, whatever is pure, whatever is lovely, whatever is gracious. . . . ' (Phil. 4:8): one of our best-loved prayers to the Holy Spirit asks that we might relish what is right. They can create a climate that encourages moral response. The basic story that anyone has about reality—about deity and self—must have profound implications for living. Our story is in the first place about God's acceptance of us just as we are. It is a story therefore which anchors us, which provides essential self-esteem—if we could believe it and receive it in our hearts and psyche. There is a deep truth in the dynamic of St John's first letter that because God has first loved us we should love one another. I do not think that is so much about gratitude or imitation as about the experience of being known and accepted—of therefore being able to accept oneself and being freed for love. It is a story that can help to banish the fear and defensiveness that make us want to read situations in terms of our own security and our own little empires. The best of our hagiographies also are stories lived in the light of Christian vision, stories of hearts grasped by the values inherent in what Christians proclaim when they come together to celebrate. It is the heart—the heart of character, the centre of choice and response—that is our problem and it is finally the heart that must be reached. It is precisely here that stories weave their magic: it is to the heart that they appeal imaginatively, giving us the reasons which we so badly need.

And yet that is not enough. Becoming moral is a difficult business and the obstacles are deeply intertwined in our emotional patterns. Such are not cast out by prayer alone. Our problem is how to educate and reorientate our emotions. Story, example and prayer are important, as are training and discipline. But as we survey our own lives and those of others we must have a question about the efficacy of prayer alone to alter moral habits. One meets people who pray much, who frequent the sacraments but who ask despairingly why it is that they are still so narrow, so unloving, so troublesome to themselves and to others. It is not bad will that is the problem but the tangled undergrowth of character. What we need perhaps is a wider notion of the grace of God abroad in the world. We need to see grace in the human.

It is the constricting effect of our emotions that prevents us from taking our great stories to heart, from opening out to others and seeing them as gift rather than as threat. Hopes for moral growth then must be aimed in that direction. Everything that delivers us from the shackles of fear, hurt, insecurity and wayward needs frees us to be moral. There is a variety of gifts in the community that facilitates that. That is to think mainly of the individual and this chapter has been about the individual, the moral agent, and the dynamics of his/her response. But there have been suggestions that it is not possible to understand the psychic wounds which inhibit that response without taking account of the social and economic conditions in which it has to be made. Some people, we said earlier, have cruel luck in life. But cruel luck is often the result of the cruel structures which alienate, which breed resentment and which push people into cheap pleasures. Programmes that try to transform consciousness, that lift people out of the passivity of hopelessness, that enable them to involve themselves in their structures and in their future are allies of morality. So too everything that respects equality, that creates justice, that takes people in from the margins. And everything that encourages self-esteem, that lifts depression, that kindles hope. All of that, of course, is kingdom-making. It is part of the programme that Jesus is recounted as announcing for himself in the fourth chapter of the Gospel according to Luke. It is the wider grace.

The Christian story implies a call to moral conversion. The Church that I know best sees that as a priority. Much of its energy goes into a concern for the orthodoxy of moral teaching. The task of teaching lies heavy on it and dictates, I suspect, much of its pastoral policy—is this the rationale for Catholic schools? All of that certainly has its place. But the task is broader and more delicate. The weight of effort has gone into telling people what is right, what to do. Fair enough. But can we concern ourselves more with enabling them to do it? That will mean moving into strategies aimed at healing the wounds which cripple response. It will mean more radically a concern with the structures which contribute to causing those wounds, an engagement in the struggle to humanise society. That, of course, should not be foreign to the Church. It is 'a constitutive dimension of the preaching of the Gospel or, in other words, of the Church's mission for the redemption of the human race. . . . ' (Synod document, *Justice in the World*, 1971)

7

SOME PROBLEM AREAS

1. Absolutes and Objectivity

I thought I would take a closer look at some issues which have
arisen obliquely in the last few chapters. The first concerns the
area of absolutes/exceptions to moral rules and of objectivity.
If you enter into discussion with any group of Christians about
morality today you will almost certainly be asked about
absolutes. I am not sure why this arises so quickly or so consistently. But it is clearly a great concern. It has to do, I think,
on the one hand with a conviction that traditionally some
moral rules have been too inflexible and on the other with a
fear that if you do not hold for moral absolutes you undermine
morality—and Church discipline.

There is often confusion about absolutes and objectivity in
morals: people are accused sometimes of not believing in
objective morality when they are raising questions about the
rather different issue of absolutes. I take it to be the case that
one believes in the objectivity of morals who believes that there
are right or at least wrong answers to moral questions, that
they arise from the way we are in the world and that such
answers apply to all similar cases. I say at least wrong answers
because there could be many right answers. There are different
styles of good Christian living—the married and single states
are obvious examples. There are also ideal and less than ideal
but still good responses to individual moral situations. But if
you hold that there are solutions to individual moral issues
that are not morally acceptable then you believe in the
objectivity of morals. This means that you do not accept that
everything is fine provided one thinks that one is doing right.
Nor do you accept that it does not matter much what in fact
one does provided one does it out of love—as some writers

associated with the Situation Ethics movement in the sixties seemed to hold. For example the statement 'If a lie is told unlovingly it is wrong, evil; if it is told in love it is good, right' (Joseph Fletcher, *Situation Ethics,* p.45) is at least open to that interpretation.

We have said earlier that people are limited in what they can see and do and that in the end what matters about an individual is how he/she in the depths of his/her heart responds to the call of goodness. It is in the secret depths of that personal response that salvation lies. However, it is a condition of genuine response that one seeks to find the truth about living. Nevertheless we all get it wrong sometimes: we arrive at wrong judgments about moral issues. That is understandable. But a community cannot simply settle for that. It must try to set out what it believes to be the morally right—the objectively right. So we can say that it was objectively wrong to send millions to the gas chambers—whatever Hitler thought.

And we particularly want to say also that it would be wrong to do so in the future. There are in fact principles of conduct, of objective morality, set out by many of our institutions, for example by the United Nations and by the Catholic Church. (Whether individuals or groups live up to them is another matter—what concerns us here is that they acknowledge that there is right and wrong conduct.) It is an important function of society to set out moral standards, to try to educate morally. Those who in all good faith get things wrong are not helping society much. With the best will in the world we can add to the confusion and irrationality of the situation and make choices more difficult for those who have to live with or who follow us.

How exactly a society or institution is proposing its moral standards—with what degree of fixity or flexibility—is a further but obviously related matter. It may be proposing them as ideals or as generally valid rules or as absolute rules. The word 'absolute' admits of several different meanings. If you ask me about a particular case—let us say that you find yourself in a situation where telling a slanderous untruth about another would bring you financial gain—I would say that it is wrong to tell the untruth. I can say that it is absolutely wrong to tell it: I mean that there are no two ways about it. But that is not what people generally have in mind when they ask about absolutes. They are asking further whether one can make a completely *general* statement about particular kinds of behaviour, whether one can say that it is always morally wrong, for example, to tell an untruth—for everybody and in all possible circumstances. Or to put it in another way, whether telling an untruth is intrinsically evil. Or to put it in still another way, whether one can say that there is no exception to the rule that one should not tell untruths. The question arises sharply in Catholic morality certainly not only about untruths but about suicide, pre-marital sex, divorce, abortion, masturbation, 'artificial' contraception, etc. Rules about them are regarded as universal rules by the tradition—that is, as always wrong in all circumstances and as absolute in this quite different sense. To avoid confusion let us refer to absolute rules of this type as universal rules.

We have seen briefly in Chapter·4 that it is possible to talk about morality at different levels. Let us develop that a bit. Take some examples: (a)—You should do good and avoid evil. (b)—You should respect others/be just, etc. (c)—You should not commit murder. (d)—You should not take your own life/You should not have sexual relations with another's spouse. All these statements give some kind of guidance about behaviour. They obviously range from very general to more particular guidance. Unless we sort out these different levels it is difficult to deal with the question of universals (absolutes): the more general one remains in moral discourse the easier it is to make an unqualified statement.

I expect that every normal person will agree on statement (a). Statements of type (b) we have already met. They say something about the general thrust of moral life. We have many such statements in our tradition—exhortations to love, fraternity, justice, respect for life, care for the young and defenceless, etc. They are very important to us. They are broad directives but they are not empty: they indicate the general direction of right living. How one is to realise them in the concrete is a further question. They do not give precise rules of guidance. A surgeon might put to you the case that a new-born baby is very seriously deformed and that even with a multitude of difficult operations its life expectancy will be very limited and the quality of its life very diminished. If he/she asks you what right conduct would be, you do not help very much if you say that he/she should respect or love the child, or should be just to the child. How? What does loving or respecting or being just involve here? You have not told him/her precisely what is right.

A principle such as (c) 'Do not ever commit murder' is not entirely clear either. The hidden question is: what qualifies as murder? We know that the statement has in mind to outlaw the wanton taking of human life and as such it is a useful bulwark in a society. But it is not wholly satisfactory to enunciate the principle 'murder is wrong' if I cannot tell you exactly what I mean by murder. Is it murder to kill a dictator? Is it murder to wage guerilla war against and kill the troops or police of an unjust government? Is it murder to attack an enemy's military position in war knowing that civilians will also be killed? One has seen car stickers 'Abortion is murder'. Is it? Is it murder to abort in situations where otherwise mother and child will die? 'Murder' seems to mean unjustified killing of a human being. But therein lies the problem: it appears to be a tautology; it is saying that unjustified killing is wrong. Still it is an important stance for a society.

There is not much problem about stating and subscribing to universals of types *a, b, c.* Most people will agree that one should always avoid moral evil/be just/avoid murder. It is not about such that the problem arises. The real nitty-gritty of the problem of universals comes with rules of kind *d.* Here you have come down to the concrete. There is unambiguous reference to a piece of behaviour without any qualifications such as 'unjustified' smuggled in. It is indisputably clear what behaviour you are telling people to avoid. For example, we know clearly what suicide, pre-marital sex or adultery refer to. Can you make universal statements involving precise descriptions of pieces of behaviour like these? Can you say that it could *never* be right to commit suicide or adultery or engage in pre-marital sex—or tell an untruth or perform a sterilisation or use contraceptives—no matter what the circumstances? Another way of looking at the matter is this: how successful will your moral rules be; will they be able to cover and be valid for all possible circumstances so that one can happily say that it will always be wrong to perform this piece of behaviour? Or if you wish to cast your morality in the form of love, can you say that there are types of behaviour that can never qualify as loving?

Rules translate values into precise concrete behaviour. The problem is that life presents us with complexity: situations do not come to us with single values or single moral considerations. Sometimes there appears to be a conflict of obligations. You are harbouring some innocent civilians and the secret police come enquiring at your door intent on taking their victims away to torture and death. You want to protect life, love others, defend justice. You also want to be truthful in life. One can go on forever declaring one's adherence to *all* these values in the abstract. But in this concrete case what is one to do? May one, should one subordinate the value of truth to the other values and tell a straight untruth in this and in all similar cases? Or is one—as some would have it—to enshrine one's adherence to truth in a rule: 'Never tell an untruth'? There is no question here of your wanting to be immoral or seeking an easy way out. You want to be faithful to the moral call but it seems to call you in different directions—to protect the life of the innocent and to be truthful. Those who raise issues about universals (absolutes) or about intrinsic evil are trying to face this complexity.

It helps, I think, to see that this is a very old question in philosophy. Plato acknowledged that one should return to others what belongs to them but asked what is to be done in the situation where you have a sword belonging to a mad man. Thomas Aquinas took up the same example: are you to return something to a person who will use it against your country? The problem is that rules are shorthand. It would be difficult to write them out in full: the result is that many admit of exceptions as they stand. Our tradition has always accepted this with regard to some rules: the question is whether it should not have extended it to others. Take killing. It is a very serious matter to kill another: it is hard to think of anything more serious. And yet everyone knows that the tradition accepted that it was permissible to execute a criminal, to kill if necessary in order to protect one's life against unjust aggression, or in a just war. In fact the standard moral manual went further and held that it is permissible to kill in defence of one's virtue or even in defence of property which is very dear to one. So if you were to state the traditional Roman Catholic position in full you would have to say: 'You may not kill except in the following circumstances....' That would be very unwieldy and moreover one could never be sure that all possible exceptions had been covered.

The question that is raised is whether there may not be exceptions to other traditional rules. It is not difficult to think up dilemmas about them. We have seen one about truth—different versions of that arise every day—and about killing. Or, you are a young married couple with a number of children and have excellent reasons why you should not have another: is your case an exception to the general rule about contraception? You are a young couple, have no hope of having a child by ordinary means and believe that having one is very important to your marriage: would your case justify *in vitro* fertilisation in the so-called simple case? A patient slowly dying in dreadful pain asks you, the doctor, to put an end to his/her life: are you justified in doing so? A soldier trapped in a blazing tank and facing a horrific death asks a companion to shoot him: may he?—is this an exception? May he shoot himself? And so on: can one think of any possible circumstances where adultery or pre-marital sex would be justified? I simply offer cases. They are obviously cases of different gravity.

To hold that a rule is universal or exceptionless or that a piece of behaviour is intrinsically evil commits one to holding that the value which your rule protects is the highest value of all, that there can never be circumstances in which there will be a clash between it and another value. Or it commits you to holding that all of the core values—truth, life, etc.—are equally basic so that there can be no subordination of one to another. We have seen that there is an irreconcilable difference between theologians on the point.

There are theologians, as we have seen, who hold that one may never directly act against a value. For such there will be several universals (absolutes). But there are many others who find it difficult to accept this and who are hesitant about declaring moral universals. Proportionalists accept that the determining factor always is the preponderant good or that one rule may yield to another. They believe that there are situations of conflict and that in them one ought to follow the more important rule (or good) even though it means going against a rule that one would normally (outside of this situation) follow. How does one know which rule is the more important? Just as one knew in the first place that, for example, life and truth *are* human values so one knows that life is a more important value than truth: in a situation of conflict one could tell an untruth or take another's property if it were necessary to save life. This does not mean that such theologians are not rigorous in their positions. They insist that we have a well-defined tradition of rules. The rules are in possession, so to speak: one must begin from them. It should be presumed that the rules indicate the right behaviour and one who claims that his/her situation is an exception must be able to demonstrate what feature of the situation makes it an exception.

It is of the very nature of rules that they apply to lots of different people in different locations etc. To hold for the validity of rules is to hold that situations are similar in moral respects, that while they obviously differ one from another physically they are similar in morally relevant respects. This differs again from the position of some of the Situation Ethics school which holds that rules are an 'intrinsicalist morass', which doubts 'if there are ever enough cases enough alike to validate a law' and which concludes that 'anything and everything is right or wrong according to the situation' (Fletcher, *Situation Ethics*, pp. 55, 124).

Proportionalists make the point that rules are of different weight or importance depending on the value which they encapsulate, and that there are some rules so rooted in human nature that it is hard to think of situations which would justify not observing them. So they will say that some rules are for all practical purposes universals (adultery is an obvious example). But they do not wish to close off the theoretical possibility that there might arise situations—perhaps quite bizarre situations—in which such rules would have to yield to more weighty considerations. As one might expect, there are some theologians who adopt a middle position, who would say that there are very few universals (rape, torture and judicial execution are mentioned) but that otherwise rules must yield to a more important rule or good.

Many people are nervous of anything less than universals (absolutes) because they feel that to speak of exceptions is to open the field wide to all kinds of licence—and this is understandable. Those with special responsibility may feel that the whole fabric of morality will ravel if the teaching authority is not strong on universals: highly organised systems do not easily tolerate exceptions. But to say that some rules admit of exceptions is not to say that they are not important and valid rules but that they may not be always adequate to the complexities of life. We have to educate ourselves to cope with that complexity. There is no reason for thinking that God is more glorified by universals than by more nuanced moral statements. Church authorities must help and trust the faithful to make mature decisions. One result of authoritarianism in morals is that some people still think that all is well if they can wangle a favourable view from one of their clergy (what the text books used to call a position in favour of liberty). They must be dissuaded from this kind of abdication of responsibility. Just as the Church cannot make behaviour moral or immoral neither can it relieve one of moral duty. The weight of responsibility must be allowed to rest where it should rest—on each individual's shoulders.

When one has said all that, much remains to be said. I have merely given the bare bones of a most complex issue. It shades into further difficulties about the distinction between doing and allowing, between being the cause of something and its occasion, and into the obscure matter of how one circumscribes a moral act. To pursue these refinements would take us too far afield but some aspects of them will necessarily arise in the following section. There is the further difficulty of definition. We have seen the problem with a word like 'murder'. Lying is another good example. Many eminent thinkers in the history of the Church have held that it is always wrong to tell an untruth—whatever the good which it might bring or the evil which it might avert. That proved to be too rigid, so theologians and people generally had recourse to the notorious notion of mental reservation or equivocation: the crude rule simply did not make sense. Others avoided the issue by redefining a lie not as intentionally telling another what one believes to be untrue (in order to deceive him/her) but as intentionally deceiving one who does not have a right to the truth in a particular instance. This, of course, permits one to say that telling a lie is always wrong. But it hides the reality that one holds in fact that there are some instances where telling an untruth is regarded as acceptable—namely, when another has not a right to the truth. How this phrase is to be cashed is now the problem. The definition of terms is therefore important.

You do not know a person's position until you know how he/she understands key terms such as 'lie', 'murder' etc. But it should be clear that no matter how terms are defined the problem of universals (absolutes) does not go away.

2. The Principle of Double Effect

Recent controversies in Ireland—especially the referenda about contraception, abortion and divorce—have pitched us as a community into very complex moral issues and forced us to take account of some of the niceties of theological argument. Even the abstruse principle of double effect raised its head in the abortion debate and we cannot be sure that we have heard the last of it. (For those who are unaware of what I am referring to, the Irish people were faced with and voted for the following amendment to their Constitution in 1983: 'The State acknowledges the right to life of the unborn and, with due regard to the equal right to life of the mother, guarantees by its laws to respect, and, as far as practicable, by its laws to defend and vindicate that right'.)

The principle of double effect has its source in the insight that there is a difference—to take one example—between aiming at a person's death because it is wanted in itself or as part of one's purpose and acting in a situation where one needs to do something quite different from killing (for example dealing with pain or with a pathological condition such as cancer), which action has the effect of the death of another. In the latter case, of course, it has to be said that one foresaw the death (often at least), was the cause of it, permitted it, and that without one's action the death would not have happened. One way of describing the difference between the two cases is to refer to them as direct and indirect killing. The question to be asked is how much difference the distinction makes in the moral assessment of cases. Our natural sense seems to say that there is a difference. But it could be that in a particular instance additional factors might modify, blur or altogether dissolve the difference.

The distinction is widely appealed to in Church teaching—for example in abortion, sterilisation, the administration of drugs etc. It says that you may not perform a direct abortion or direct sterilisation, or directly kill a dying patient.

But you may remove a fallopian tube or cancerous womb although this causes the death of the foetus, perform surgery for some medical condition that has the effect of sterilisation, administer drugs for the relief of pain that have the effect of shortening life, engage in a just war knowing that one causes the death of innocent non-combatants, resist an unjust aggressor even to the point of his/her death.

Cases of this kind are usually gathered under the principle of double effect, which is an attempt to give a general formula to cover situations where there are good and bad effects of a single action. The standard statement of the principle is that it is legitimate to perform an act on which two effects follow with equal immediacy, one good and the other bad, if four conditions are fulfilled: the act in itself must be good or indifferent; the evil effect must not be intended; the good effect must not come through the evil effect; and there must be a proportionate reason for causing the harm. The principle is often summed up in the saying that a good end does not justify an evil means.

Whether the principle validly encapsulates our sense of the distinction of direct and indirect and whether it can be applied to quite varying situations where there is a good and bad effect involved is in question. The principle is rarely found outside of Catholicism, is often indeed referred to as the Roman Catholic principle of double effect and there is hardly a moralist outside of Catholicism who would accept it in all its rigorous application. A growing number of Catholics are unhappy about it also. It is important to realise that the principle is not of divine origin but is a rule of thumb thought up by theologians of the past to deal with complex cases where there seems to be a clash of values. It is a useful tool but increasingly it is being found that it will not bear the weight that it is being asked to carry: one of the problems is that it is applied indiscriminately to quite different kinds of cases. Certainly many regard it as a form of hair-splitting, as unnecessarily complicating moral decisions and as sometimes leading to unacceptable conclusions. Its most controversial application is in the case of abortion. Let us look at that: it provides a good example of the problems of the principle and is, of course, of continuing interest. It was a matter of crucial importance in the 1983 referendum debate: in fact the very distinction which is at the heart of the principle was incorporated into some definitions of abortion—we will come to that in a moment.

The Catholic position is that if a pregnant woman is in danger from some potentially fatal condition such as a heart condition which can be relieved only by termination of the pregnancy it is morally wrong—it is in effect murder—to abort the foetus. (It may be, as some gynaecologists hold, that such cases do not ever arise now. But the 1983 referendum debate was evidence that medical opinion in this country is divided on the matter. Even if the cases are only hypothetical they help to test the principle and its validity.) It is maintained that in this case the death of the foetus is intended, that it is being directly killed and that its death is the evil means to the good end of the preservation of the life of the mother. Similarly, the Church forbade craniotomy in situations of difficult delivery, when such cases were a problem, even if it was the only means to save the life of the mother. However the Church does accept as morally permissible the removal of a cancerous womb or of a diseased fallopian tube in pregnancy cases even though the death of the foetus is foreseen and certain. Here, it is said, the act in question is not a direct attack on the foetus but the removal of a diseased organ, the good effect of the saving of the life of the mother does not come through the death of the foetus but through the removal of the organ, and the death of the foetus is not intended but only permitted. So there are two kinds of abortion which are morally worlds apart: one is murder, the other morally right.

In recent times there has been an attempt on the part of some Catholic moralists to redefine abortion and it occasioned some confusion in the 1983 referendum debate. Traditionally the Catholic Church has defined abortion as the removal from the womb of a living, non-viable foetus. As we have seen, it distinguished between direct and indirect abortion. That meant that not all abortion was immoral, specifically indirect abortion where there was a proportionate reason. The new strategy has been to define abortion as the direct and deliberate killing of the foetus. This does not change the substantial position but it incorporates the distinction of the principle of double effect into the very definition. It enabled the pro-life movement, as it has come to be called, to declare that all abortion is immoral and that there are no exceptions. One disturbing effect was that when an advocate of this position was asked whether the case of the cancerous womb was not an exception his reply was that this was *not an abortion* but a hysterectomy. That, while intended as an attempt to protect the foetus to the maximum extent, was, I suggest, a dangerous tactic. The definition of moral acts is a minefield in itself: to describe this act without any reference to killing or abortion is to fail to describe it adequately and is likely in the end to be counter-productive in the effort to protect life.

There are problems about nearly every point in the differentiation of direct and indirect abortion where the life of the mother is at stake. So much so that there are some who think that the application of the principle breaks down. In the ectopic pregnancy situation the general teaching held that one could morally remove the fallopian tube with the foetus inside but that to remove the foetus directly—to shell out the tube as they used to say—and try to repair the damaged tube was a direct abortion and murder. (Again, how feasible or useful this might be medically is not the crucial issue.) This position just did not make sense to reasonable people. The fact that it held that to do greater rather than less physical harm to the mother was what was morally right and that the difference between the procedure of removal and that of repair—the foetus dies in both—was that between moral legitimacy and murder shattered the confidence of many authors in the principle.

In recent years the principle has come under close scrutiny: in particular the key issue of the meaning of 'direct' and 'intend' has come in for attention. Even conservative theologians are unhappy: one has suggested that the ectopic case should be regarded as an exception to the immorality of direct abortion; another has reinterpreted the principle so as to include a broader range of cases under indirect abortion. What is important to remember is that there is no point in simply repeating the formula of the principle—saying, for example, that one act is wrong because the evil result is directly intended and another is right because it is indirectly intended. It should be kept in mind that in both cases the foetus is killed. The whole issue is to demonstrate that there is a morally significant difference in this abortion case between what is called 'direct' and what is called 'indirect'.

The fact is that there is no agreement about the meaning or

significance of 'intend' (or 'deliberate') and 'direct'. For example, does one intend—in the usual sense of the term—to kill an unjust aggressor if one finds it necessary? One does, and yet it is regarded by some as an example of the principle and as a legitimate act. Compare now the two abortion situations—(*a*) the case of the cancerous womb or fallopian tube pregnancy and (*b*) the case of the pregnant mother who has some other fatal condition which could be relieved by the termination of the pregnancy. If you asked the surgeon in case (*a*) if he intended to kill the foetus he would probably have to say 'yes and no': he certainly intended to perform an act which he foresaw would inevitably result in the death of the foetus. He wishes that he did not have to kill the foetus. But so does the surgeon in (*b*). It is also true that each has the same reason for performing the act: each wants to save the mother. One has to say further that in neither case is it precisely through the death of the foetus that the good effect is brought about. It is true that if the foetus were not present the problem would not arise in case (*b*) but even if the foetus did not die the effect would be the same: the death of the foetus is not sought; it is its removal that is important. Some theologians have great difficulty in seeing that there is a significant moral difference between the cases.

Although the 'directly/indirectly intended' distinction is crucial to the principle, moralists who defend it have found it difficult to explain. Some contend that an evil is indirectly intended if it is the unintentional by-product of an act—the agent aiming at some good effect although perhaps foreseeing that the act will also produce an evil effect. This enables them to make a distinction between morally unintended and psychologically unintended: something could be psychologically intended—in the sense of foreseen—but morally unintended. This is how they would justify the foreseen abortion of (*a*) and outlaw that of (*b*); from the point of view of the agent the death in (*a*) is an unintentional by-product of the operation on the cancerous womb or fallopian tube. Others say that an evil is indirectly intended if it is the *per accidens* result of an act, directly intended if it is the *per se* object: the emphasis here is on the nature of the act. Thus the *per se* object of the operation to remove a cancerous womb is just that, the *per accidens* effect is the death of the foetus which happens to be in the womb that is to be removed: there could be an operation to remove a cancerous womb without any question of pregnancy. And this—the difference between *per se* and *per accidens* and not that between psychologically and morally intended—is how this group would accept (*a*) and outlaw (*b*). More recently it has been suggested that an evil effect is indirect if it is part of an indivisible act of which only the good effect is intended, the evil being permitted.

Much modern opinion believes that theologians got themselves caught up in unnecessary complications. Proportionalists, as might be expected, make the point that acts of this kind involving pre-moral evil should be judged as a whole and that it is only when the totality of the human or pre-moral good is assessed that the act can be said to be morally right or wrong. (I explained the notion of pre-moral good and evil in Chapter 4. I mean by it factual or human good and evil. It is a pre-moral or factual human evil to lose a leg, a kidney or one's life. But whether it is a moral evil to remove a person's leg or kidney depends on the circumstances—they might be diseased. It is normally a moral evil to take another's life but that too depends on the circumstances: it is not immoral to shoot a mad gunman if that is the only way to prevent wholesale slaughter.) In both abortion cases the act to be described, they say, is killing or removing a living non-viable foetus the presence of which is endangering the life of the mother, with the intention of saving her life in circumstances where if this is not done both mother and foetus will die. The act, they say, must be judged in this way. They therefore object to regarding a part of the act—killing—as having a morality of its own before all the elements are weighed and consequently object to the idea that the good effect is coming through a *moral* evil. You do not know whether there is moral evil or not until you consider all the factors. (Cf. Chapter 5)

There is evil, they acknowledge—the pre-moral evil of the death of the foetus. But their general theory is that if there is proportionate reason for causing pre-moral evil—even the death of another—one may do so whether it be done directly or indirectly. There is such a reason in this case, they say, the reason being that the presence of the foetus is causing danger to the life of the mother and that both will die if the pregnancy is not terminated.

A number of points may now be made about this position. First, Proportionalists do not need to justify intervention in the cases of ectopic pregnancy and of the cancerous womb by appeal to the principle of double effect: it can be seen that they do so more straightforwardly. Second, they regard the principle as it has been elaborated by tradition as misunderstanding the nature of moral judgment and, in particular, as missing the significance of distinguishing between pre-moral and moral evil: a good end may be sought through an evil means that is only pre-morally evil. Third, if a rare case should occur in which a pregnant woman is suffering from a potentially fatal condition, let us say a heart condition, which can only be alleviated by termination of the pregnancy and which otherwise will result in the death of both, Proportionalists generally justify a direct intervention.

Some Proportionalists regard the distinction of direct and indirect action as having a relevance in judgment: they do not as easily accept a direct as an indirect causing of evil. But while the distinction is relevant for them it is not decisive—as in the case just considered. It is the presence or absence of proportionate reason that is decisive: for most Catholic moralists the only proportionate reason which could justify either the direct or indirect killing of the foetus is the saving of one of two lives.

It is important to note that such moralists do not accept just any combination of factors which will result in death as justifying abortion. Compare the cases just considered with that of an unmarried pregnant girl whose mother is suffering from a serious heart condition: according to the best medical opinion she will die from shock if she discovers her daughter's condition. I know of no Catholic moralist who would justify an abortion in such circumstances although it might be thought to bear some similarities to the earlier cases. The difference, I think, is in the relation of the pregnancy to the death of the mother. In the case of the pregnant woman who is suffering from a heart condition it is of the very nature of the physical components of the case that one's only choice is to intervene or leave both mother and foetus to die and that it is the presence of the foetus that is physically causing or aggravating the critical condition of the patient. In the case of the unmarried pregnant girl there are other things that can be done: the mother can be counselled etc. It is not the foetus who is causing the danger to the mother but her own prejudices: as things stand the life of the foetus is in danger of being subordinated to such prejudices. We can take two well-worn examples which illustrate the difference. We commend the driver of a runaway train who sees five workmen on the track on which he is travelling (and who are certain to be killed) and who manages to divert to another track where there is only one workman—I do not think we need to appeal to the complexities of the principle of double effect to do so. We do not commend the judge/sheriff (cf. Chapter 5) who is warned by a murderous gang that they will certainly kill five members of the black community if he does not execute someone for a crime which has been committed—and who frames an innocent man.

The general thrust of the principle of double effect is important. There is a difference between aiming at something and permitting it. But the elaboration of this insight into the rigid conditions of the principle and its application to a wide variety of situations has not stood up to examination. A philosopher sympathetic to the principle has had to conclude that the doctrine of its application to abortion in the situations envisaged above must conflict with that of most reasonable people.[1] As we have seen, some moralists have tried to reinterpret the principle by extending the notion of indirect abortion, by finding exceptions to the traditional doctrine of direct abortion or by following the Proportionalist line.

There is a wide variety of situations in which good and evil results seem to be simultaneously present and they present us with difficult choices. A whole plethora of distinctions has been required to deal with them—that between doing and allowing, between being the cause of something and its condition or occasion (as in the case of the mother of the pregnant girl), between positive and negative duties, between one's responsibility for what one does oneself and what others do (as in the judge/sheriff case). Above all there are the difficult situations which of their nature leave one with a choice only between greater or less evil. These difficult situations sometimes involve factors which cannot be squeezed into the rigid conditions of the principle of double effect.

Even in the case where to do nothing is to allow two deaths to occur some moralists still choose to do nothing and to preserve their personal integrity. There is behind this a certain view of God, of providence and of human tragedy: the perspective is that we should leave all to God rather than get involved in causing the great evil of killing a foetus. It is an understandable position. The other view is that to refuse to do anything in this case is a selfish policy of keeping one's own hands clean at all costs and whatever the resultant loss (two deaths), and even perhaps as morally reprehensible. It takes a different view of one's responsibility before God and notes that Church tradition does not say that one may never kill: after all indirect abortion can equally be said to involve and to cause death.

The principle was a brave effort to formulate a general principle for different complex cases. It can be said to have been a very powerful defence of human life in particular and it cannot be easily abandoned: attempts to reformulate it have not been entirely successful so far. But it is not a sacred principle and Catholic moral theory must be open to re-examine its application to particular issues. It is well to note that it is not undergirded by revelation—Christian faith has nothing substantial to say about its validity. It is a philosophical tool, must be argued for philosophically and must meet the reservations that are raised against some of its applications by moralists generally. The matter has been of some importance recently in Ireland. Some people were unhappy with the formula of the 1983 amendment: part of their fear was that behind the formula and behind the rejection of other formulae was an attempt to write into the Constitution the Catholic moral position including the controverted principle of double effect. How the formula will be interpreted in State law in relation to mother-and-child cases seems to be still a matter of some uncertainty.

The last two sections have pointed up the complexity of moral decisions. We all meet the everyday cases where there appears to be a straight clash of values. But some choices are particularly harrowing—such as the abortion cases just considered. Situations of violence and of war throw up similarly distressing cases—we know something of the agony of decision faced by many in the resistance movements and in concentration camps and one could point to problems nearer home. Some have referred to them as limit or boundary situations.

147

In general the Catholic tradition has taken the view that there is a right/wrong solution to moral problems—however difficult to discern. But recently there has been increased attention to 'the sin of the world' in Catholic writing—the tangled, sullied and corrupt setting which sometimes leaves us only with a choice that is less than ideal. There is reference to the need for a theology of compromise to meet that, one that would take into account the constrictions under which decision has to be made. Some Protestant theologians take the interesting view that an act can be both morally right or obligatory and also morally wrong. In this view human existence is so enveloped in sin that we find that we must do wrong in doing what is obligatory or right—e.g. killing a foetus in order to save one of two lives. We are, in this view, necessarily involved in guilt. (There is behind this, of course, a wider theological stance about sin and salvation.) It seems to me that considerations of this kind have something to recommend them. We cannot just glibly solve moral dilemmas by opting for the more weighty of values or the lesser of two evils or even by doing nothing without some regret at our abandonment of the lesser value or the occurrence of the evil in which we are somehow involved. Whether or not that should be called guilt I do not know, but it appears to me to be part of moral wholeness and wholesomeness to treasure all values even when one has to act against them. And that applies whether our intervention is direct or indirect.

3. Morality and Church Discipline

The Church is the community of the disciples of the Lord, the Body of Christ, the sign and sacrament of the salvation of the world. Its aim is to bear as fully as possible in its members the likeness of Christ—to be a letter written by Christ (2 Cor. 3:3)—to carry out its 'ministry of reconciliation' (2 Cor. 5:18) and to be a dynamic energy for the advent of the kingdom of peace, hope and love. It is a community which must organise itself in order to carry out its purpose. To do so it makes laws. There are a great many such laws—far too many some would say. The present Code of the law of the Church contains 1752 canons. That which was in use until recently (the 1918 Code) had 2414 and a vast amount of additional law had been promulgated since 1918.

We have laws about times, places and conditions for the celebration of baptism, confirmation, the Eucharist etc. We have laws about when you may get married, to whom, by whom, with what preparations, with what consequences; laws about schools and universities, about priestly and religious life, about lay organisations, about dispensations and indults; laws about funerals, about churches and their care, about church property, about the treatment of serious sinners, about the kind of dress and decoration which may be worn by certain people, about appointments and elections, about punishments and trials, about ecclesiastical courts, about fast days and feast days, about altars, shrines, cemeteries, about who can hear confessions and where and how, about states and rank and distinctions in the Church—and lots more. You would not have thought that the kingdom movement of the carpenter of Nazareth would have required such vast and detailed organisation.

If law has a point the point is the Gospel. It has to be judged in that light. We all have to be alive to the danger that maintaining the institution with its laws can become more important for us than remembering Christ and sharing his spirit. It is easy to miss the point: one can become a zealot for the law and miss the Gospel. But the better the laws, the more clearly they point in the direction of the Gospel, the more likely they are to be respected.

The expression, 'law of the Church' is used very loosely. The Church performs two quite different functions in the area of law and morality. It makes laws such as those just mentioned. It is right and important that it does so. But we must distinguish this law-making activity of the Church from its activity when it makes statements about morality, for example its declarations about justice or divorce. There it is performing a different function. There it purports to be telling us the truth about moral issues. Not to be making anything right or wrong, but enlightening us, giving us answers, acting as an expert on moral issues, teaching. The Church, of course, cannot affect morality, cannot make anything right or wrong. Morality is independent of it: whether something is right or wrong depends on whether or not it conforms to the criterion of morality (as it seems to me, whether it is humanising for society or not). In teaching morality the Church is giving its

149

opinion on an issue and declaring that the faithful ought to follow this because the Church thinks that it is the right interpretation of the issue. To refer to such teaching as the law of the Church is to use the term incorrectly. When people ask that the Church change its 'law' about, say, divorce or contraception (as many have asked) or about social justice (as some asked in the wake of the radical teaching of *Populorum Progressio* and subsequent documents), what they are really asking is that it change its view about the morality of such matters, that it see things differently. If it did, it would be saying that it had been wrong in its earlier teaching. It would be changing its opinion about something that is independent of it, which is quite different from changing its laws. One *could possibly* be asking something else—not that the Church revise its teaching but revise the way it treats those who act contrary to its teaching, e.g. allow the divorced and remarried to the sacraments or accept polygamists for baptism. That is more a matter of discipline.

Making Church law is a different matter from teaching morality. That is entirely within the competence of the Church itself. Of course such law cannot be arbitrary: there must be point or purpose to it. That is not to say however, that one must be able to demonstrate that a particular law is absolutely entailed by some element of Church life: it is of the nature of things that there are different possible and adequate ways of achieving the same purpose; but there must be some clear relation of the law to the end of the Church. (So—to take some recent examples—there could be several different ways of ensuring that there be reverence for the Eucharist or that the people of God practise some detachment in their lives.) Church law is human law, made by human beings: it will reflect the culture, sex, language, limitations and preoccupations of its makers. We have the guarantee of the Lord only that his essential truth will not be utterly lost in the Church: we have no such guarantee about law. Law is not made in heaven but on earth and can be changed by the same agents who made it. So in our life-time we have seen the Church change many laws about fast and abstinence, the Eucharistic fast, the obligation of Sunday Mass, conditions for the reception of sacraments, religious life, the promises to be made in a mixed marriage, attendance at services of other Churches etc.

There is a general moral obligation on us to contribute to

the well-being of the Church so that the mission of Christ may be accomplished through it and therefore a moral obligation to respect its laws. We must situate law in terms of its meaning, purpose and necessity for the life of the Church. The principle has been accepted always that such law does not bind if it involves disproportionate inconvenience—that is something that is to be measured against such purpose and necessity. That is sometimes built into the law itself: those who for reasons outside their control could not have the canonical form of marriage, for example, could simply marry one another without it. In the past, theologians and canonists were much too ready to regard disobedience to Church law as a serious matter—as mortal sin—so that nowadays you sometimes have people asking how someone could be regarded as having been condemned to hell for the violation of a law of abstinence that has now been abolished. The very fact that law has changed has brought about a rethink: if the Church can do away with such laws can they have been so crucial to the life of the community that disobedience involved the catastrophic consequences threatened by theologians?

You might ask how many more laws will be changed. A question that is becoming more topical is: who should be involved in such change? Do the millions of Christians around the world sit idly by until some officials of the Curia get the idea that it would be good to change a law? Or should they be making their views known about what kind of laws best serve the kingdom of God and having an active part in the process of change? They should. To the extent that the making and changing of law is confined to a small group of officials to that extent will it lack respect. We had the revelation some time ago that the Irish hierarchy had thought of asking Rome to change the law on mixed marriage, because of our particular circumstances, but had desisted because they felt that it would be pointless going to Rome. That is a very strange state of affairs. There is the more scandalous issue of the non-involvement of women in law-making—even in laws made for women. I quote Monika Hellwig—her remarks refer not only to law but to the interpretation of morality: 'There is a manifest absurdity in the pretence that this discernment is done better and is more likely to respond to God's will if women are excluded from the reflections or at least from drawing conclusions'.[2]

But while we distinguish statements about morality from the making of laws there are areas where the line of distinction is not clear and where apparently insoluble problems arise. This is particularly so about marriage because it is a human institution with its own autonomy but something about which the Church lays down conditions. For centuries the Church simply accepted the human institution and did not make laws about it. Marriage is a relationship entered into by two people: this commitment or bond is the heart of the matter and it is out of it that their moral relationship essentially arises. But the Church says that some marriages are valid and others not. Suppose two people make the core commitment but do not meet something required solely by the Church for validity. What is their condition: are they married? If the question, 'Are they married' asks whether they are regarded by the Church as married then obviously they are not. But if it asks about their relationship to one another and whether they are in the same condition as two single people then it can hardly be said that they are. Discipline and morality do not coincide.

Take the situation where one has moral certainty that his/her marriage is invalid but cannot get a decree of nullity through Church courts—we all know that it is not always possible to adduce compelling evidence and that some courts are more difficult than others. Again discipline and morality do not coincide: the Church makes moral judgments about such a person; it forbids him/her to marry, regards him/her as living in sin if marriage is attempted and children of the new union as born out of wedlock. The corollary is also true. One might have obtained a decree of nullity knowing full well that one did not have a genuine case: the Church treats the person as free to marry but that has no effect on the moral status of the parties or on their responsibilities to one another. And what is one to make of the marriage of priests who cannot now get a dispensation which they would have got a few years ago? The unions into which they have entered would then have been regarded as moral: now they are regarded as immoral. How does this accident of history affect the couple's moral status? This is not to say that the public ordering of marriage is not important or that it does not have its own moral implications. It is to point to the inadequacy of law to deal totally with the commitment of marriage.

In the early chapters of this book we tried to sort out the complex relationships between autonomous morality and religion. Here we find further complexities. The discipline of the Church itself introduces new moral considerations. The discipline at times also determines the moral status which an individual will be regarded as having in the community. It will treat him/her and make judgments about his/her behaviour accordingly. These are delicate matters and a Church community could hardly be too sensitive. Morality has a life of its own and the moral condition of an individual is not always transparent to human judgment. We need to be able to make distinctions about these matters.

However there is no use yearning for the dewy-fresh days of the early Church. The charismatic movement of Jesus Christ has become a world wide organisation and it needs laws in order to keep its life vibrant. But we all need to be aware of the limitations of discipline and of its curious interplay with morality. We have true authorities in the Church. We can only hope that they will be wise, that the very human process of law-making will be as participative as possible and that it will safeguard and facilitate the life of Christ in us. The early disciples were bold enough to say about their decisions, 'It has seemed good to the Holy Spirit and to us....' (Acts 15.28): it will remain a challenge to the Church for all time to listen sensitively to what the Spirit is saying.

8

THE APPEAL TO CONSCIENCE

WE hear much about conscience—'the voice of conscience', 'the rights of conscience', 'informing conscience', 'consulting conscience', 'following conscience'. Conscience is made to look like a special faculty or piece of equipment which we possess. If that is the image we have then the most useful thing we could say about conscience is that there is no such thing.

In a sense we have been referring to conscience all through this book. We have agreed that we are conscious of the moral dimension of life. We are aware that right and good living with others makes a claim on us, that there is a truth to be realised in living, that there are objects, ends, goods—values—to be sought. We know that life cannot (that 'cannot' again) be lived simply for profit or pleasure but according to some other criterion. That awareness is conscience. It is consciousness of the moral call that is in question. One is conscious of lots of other things, of course. But we are concentrating here on moral consciousness, awareness of oneself as a being with a moral path to follow. It is not so much that I have a conscience—a special piece of equipment—as that I am a conscience. That is how I am, that is how I find myself. That is a basic truth about life.

You could tease this out into different strands. My 'conscience' as I sit at this typewriter can refer to the fact that I experience the moral dimension of life but it can be extended to the set of moral principles that I have. So if I say that my conscience will not allow me to do something while yours might, I do not mean that I have a moral sense and you do not but that I interpret some issues differently from you—perhaps you see capital punishment as acceptable and I do not, or I regard telling untruths as sometimes acceptable and you do not. By further extension I might say that someone has a sensitive conscience: I mean that he/she (rightly) sees moral issues where others (with a more lax conscience) crudely bash ahead. Or I might refer to a scrupulous conscience: I mean that a person tends not to be able to solve moral issues well because of some underlying anxiety.

'Conscience' is used to refer backwards and forwards. You will hear people say, 'My conscience reproaches (or troubles) me'. They are conscious of not having acted as they know they should have or of having acted in a particular way when they were not sure if it was morally acceptable. But 'conscience' most commonly refers to judgment about an issue that is arising, that confronts me now.

Many associate conscience with feelings: of remorse, probably, but perhaps also of joy—the joy of a good conscience. That is not surprising. The moral dimension of life is a serious matter for us. It grasps us deeply. It is of much greater import than other kinds of achievement. It is what most truly determines us as persons. We suggested that life in accordance with it is what we most deeply want. It is not surprising then that moral consciousness has a heavy emotional concomitant. One cannot ignore it without far-reaching effects in the psyche, without feelings of guilt: one who listens to it knows an inner peace even when it calls for difficult and painful decisions. We do no service to ourselves or others if we airbrush out feelings of guilt. Guilt is healthy and proper provided it is appropriate, i.e., guilt for real fault measured to the seriousness of the fault. But there is inappropriate guilt. We carry a lot of baggage of guilt and fear from childhood attaching to actions that the mature and rational person would not regard as wrong or at least not as seriously wrong. A nagging remorse demands to be assuaged and we may go along with it for the sake of our peace. That is no solution: we may need counsel to free ourselves from such pseudo-morality and reach the clear light of a strong and sensitive conscience.[1]

When we address the issue of conscience we are not moving into new territory. The material of earlier chapters, especially that on the agent, is relevant. We all have some kind of conscience or moral consciousness. But in line with what we said earlier some expressions of it can only be analogously called conscience. Much is made of the fact that a very small child has a sense of things to be done and avoided. But it is highly debatable whether this has much to do with morality. What command and prohibition mean for the child differ greatly from what they mean for a person of mature conscience: it is a different entity. The kind of conscience which a person can have (the kind of judgments which he/she is capable of and what such judgments mean) is in the first place a matter of age. The young are incapable of appropriating, of taking to themselves, of accepting freely the claim that being-with-others makes on us. They have not yet come to experience the human need for a way of life founded on impartiality, justice and perhaps even on sacrifice for the other. But even with adults the quality of conscience differs greatly.

A RESPONSIBLE CONSCIENCE

A genuine personal conscience is not presented to us by life as a gift and is not by any means an automatic attainment. It has to be forged in the smithy of the individual's soul. We said that moral consciousness is affected by factors both outside our control and within it. It is affected by the 'givens' of life and by how we responded to such 'givens'. To some extent our particular kind of conscience is made for us because we absorb so much of the point of view, values and prejudices of our culture and background. We may be lucky or unlucky. To some other extent we make our own conscience as we act on the 'givens' of life. How we arrived at the moral consciousness that now is ours is each one's story. (It would be a brave person who would judge just how responsible we are for who we have become.) I am not just referring to the correctness of our judgments, the set of principles by which we operate (conscience in that material sense) but to the whole inner sense of moral responsibility, to the free and deliberate taking on (or otherwise) of the task of creating one's moral self. Here too the quality of conscience can greatly vary.

As in other areas we must again keep before us both the ideal and the reality. What we are looking for is authentic response to the experience of life. The ideal is not that consciousness be a receptacle that passively receives accurate information and accepts answers from without, but that it be a principle of

156

operations, a self that accepts the responsibility of freedom. Genuine morality, we said before, requires genuine humanness and the developed conscience can only be one that measures up to personal maturity and autonomy. That is ideally the conscience of a person who is aware of responsibility, who has taken on the burden of existence, who has achieved the openness to look steadily at the facts, who having moved from self-interest to love of others is able to respond to values. Such a character will achieve objectivity in judgment and both rightness and goodness in action.

There are three foci here. First, there is the appropriation of one's existence, the ready acceptance that life has to be chosen and that what has to be chosen above all is responsibility for one's self, for what one makes. This in contradistinction to a life that is an uncritical conformity to a moral code given by an external authority—and even more so to a life of drift or one governed by human respect. Vatican II recommended 'a more mature and personal exercise of liberty' (*The Church in the Modern World*, n.6) and referred to 'those internal, voluntary and free acts whereby man sets the course of his life directly toward God' and is 'privileged to bear personal responsibility' (*Declaration on Religious Freedom*, nn.3, 2). Conformity will not work anyway. Life is too varied and situations too various to be captured in rules. To be immobilised and limited by them is a failure in maturity.

Second, there is the self-transcendence, (the willingness to go beyond one's own interests,) involved in the honest quest for the truth about one's situations—and that requires an unselfishness. Even to want to know, even to begin to care presumes an unselfishness. There is involved not just the honesty to look with both concern and detachment but a sensibility and imagination that searches what one should say or do to and for another and how and when—and if. Making ethical judgments is in some fashion about imagining alternatives. And not just about one other but about groups—what is appropriate for them, what is growth-making, peace-making, community-building. And not just about groups but about the larger society, about all who will be affected by one's action or inaction—another community perhaps, another country, those who produce what we buy and eat (are they getting a fair price for their produce?) those whose livelihood depends on what we do or how we vote, those affected by our life-styles, even future generations and their environment.

That concern presumes the third focus—that one cares, that one has been affectively converted in some sense, that the habitual object of one's desires is not personal gratification but what serves others. We return to the old problem: is one free enough of fears, seductions and selfish desires to be able to look honestly, to be objective. We have pointed already to the close relationship between love of goodness and right knowledge. Objectivity in morals is not 'out there': it is in correct subjectivity, in true judgment which presupposes an openness and an ability to read situations. But are we able for that? Freedom, Iris Murdoch says, is not strictly the exercise of the will but rather the experience of accurate vision which, when this becomes appropriate, occasions action: that involves freedom from fantasy and from a host of blinding, self-centred aims and images.[2] And so Aquinas too says that it is only the good person, the virtuous one, who is prudent, i.e. capable of good judgments and choices.

That is the ideal, what must be hoped for. The reality is that most of us live our lives well short of the ideal. We fail perhaps in the human task of taking on our lives consciously and purposively. We drift. We go along with the crowd. We allow life to wash up against us rather than setting before ourselves the project of living. The achievement of personal autonomy or responsibility is not just or not primarily a religious matter—much modern philosophy has concerned itself with it—but it has religious implications. If the glory of God is the person fully alive, then a Christian life that is marked by critical human awareness must be of more value than one that is passive. (This, let it be said, is not a matter of intelligence but of presence to oneself: the technically uneducated can be full of life.)

It is for this reason that the Church must welcome the emergence of a critical questioning laity who will follow that fundamental human urge that is sometimes referred to as 'the unrestricted desire to know'; who will not be put off by specious reasons or arguments; who will not say, 'Whatever you say yourself, Father', or 'Yes, of course' when they are in no way convinced; who will see fallacies where there are fallacies. To ask people to bury their questioning and intelligence is no service to humanity and can be no service to God and religion. The old scholastic dictum that grace builds on nature must mean that an adult, critical and restless desire for the truth will not deceive or betray us and cannot be an infidelity to faith. We have become more educated and a certain demythologising must take place about religion and morality. A laity that does not think for itself on such matters inevitably encourages a creeping infallibility. This is in no way to suggest that there is not place for faith and guidance. But we must be honest: one cannot be asked to bury genuine reservations; honest doubt is preferable to naivete or pretence.

Forming conscience cannot be just a matter of following what we are told to do. We have to decide about the particulars of our lives. Moral tradition is crudely stated: 'You shall not kill', 'You shall not steal'. Even if it were stated with some refinement, that would not absolve one from the individual judgment that must be made. For example if the moral *rule* is that one may take the property of another if one cannot otherwise avoid death, the judgment must be made that these are *in fact* the circumstances in which one finds oneself. If a law does not bind where it involves undue inconvenience one must judge whether there is *in fact* undue inconvenience—that is, whether or not one's particular case falls under what is envisaged by the law. By their very nature such decisions can be made only by the person confronted with them. No one can be deputised to make them. No one else can make them in one's stead. There can be no automatic application of moral rules in the situation: there is always required the creative and critical judgment. We have seen that one may judge that one's case is an exception to the general rule.

There is another reason why forming conscience cannot be just a matter of what we are told: because the rules—commandments—which have been most prominent in the tradition tell us only a minimum. To limit moral life to that would have the effect of limiting the range of the moral. Our moral lives, we said earlier, are not just about the Ten Commandments. They are about the particularities of life in the fields and streets where we work and play, love and hate, plan and create, give and receive—in occasions for fidelity or infidelity, for grasping or giving, for community building or self promotion, for envying or encouraging, for resenting or praising, for exploiting or being of service, for quiet devotion or noisy seeking of notice. To such situations we have to respond. We have to decide what should be done and what we can do: decisions of conscience are in part also about our personal possibilities and potentialities.

DIFFICULTIES

What I have said so far is about our form or style of conscience or consciousness. But we fail too, if fail is the word—I suppose it is—in content. We fail in the sense that we get it wrong. People end up with a firm conviction that a course of action is right when it is in fact wrong. (What I mean by that I'll come to in a minute.) That is the clear case: we are quite convinced and quite wrong. But there are so many areas of grey. We approach so many of our decisions with an undeveloped, because clouded, intelligence and under the doubtful guidance of an incomplete willingness. To have the candid openness of the morally converted, the vulnerable generosity of one who has passed from self-interest to other-centredness, is for most of us more an aspiration than a reality. So we reach most of our decisions in the half light—half seeking the truth because half willing. (And the less developed one is morally, the less one appreciates the need for development.) We rationalize and hide from the truth. We half-convince and half-persuade ourselves. We become the easy prey of our fears and anxieties. Most of us, I suspect, live our lives in that shadowland.

But it is a pity if we get it wrong: it is bad for ourselves, for the world, for the kingdom. Every falling short in willingness and in understanding is a pity. It is a failure in the art of living. But we do get things wrong and it is not surprising. Quite apart from the weakness that all flesh is heir to we are faced with situations—both common and particular—that are complex and opaque. It is just not easy to know what is the loving or humanising way. About justice issues, about fair distribution, about the significance of a job, about the relation between effort and reward, about incentives for investment and entrepreneurship, about pay differentials, about just reward for different types of work (clerical, manual, family, professional), about more jobs or better jobs, about fair trading, nuclear deterrents, care of the environment, revolution, IVF, homo-sexual relations, divorce. About issues of law and morality, freedom of the press, terminal illness. That is just to mention some very public issues. So, not surprisingly, there is sincerely held difference of opinion about such matters, as we see every day.

Even more so is there complexity or opaqueness in the unique circumstances of the individual's life—as we mentioned already in Chapter 3. What should one do? Should I separate from my cruel husband who abuses me and my children? Should I put my mother/mother-in-law in a home where she will be lonely but at least safe and comfortable? To what extent should I give my adolescent children freedom to read and see what they like or try to protect and censor their activities? Should husband or wife give up work so as to look after the children better? Should we have another baby? Should the priest who no longer believes in the priesthood get out of it and give up the ministry? Should the sister who is a constant source of friction and upset for the community leave? Cases having their own personal contours, not entirely describable in terms of any other case.

In the common and, especially, public issues difference of viewpoint is hardly desirable in principle. It betokens a failure of our common intelligence. But difference is a reality of living together in a world that presents us with complex prob-lems—although St Paul seemed to think that the Christian spirit could lead us to a happy common discernment—and to that we must respond both as individuals and in matters of public policy. We have to make room for sincerely held difference of opinion. The danger is of taking refuge in jargon such as, 'Error has no rights'. The issues to be faced are: what are the implications for our own actions—and for our sal-vation—of the fact that we err; how are we to regard (what is the moral way of regarding) those who differ from us; how are institutions such as Church and State to treat conscientious dissenters?

A preliminary point is the very statement that people make wrong judgments. Wrong by what standards? Who says they are wrong? For anyone to say so may appear an arrogance but it is only to say that there *are* true values and therefore right and wrong judgments and choices. I suggested earlier that we might think of the history of the race as a search for such truths. Hitler may have thought that he was right and there are well-documented cases of maniac killers who believed that they had divine authorisation. Indeed there is no shortage in the history of the Church of authorities who thought that they were justified in some injustice or cruelty from which Christians nowadays would want to distance themselves. We believe that such people were wrong in their judgments. So we find ourselves forced to say that they thought they were right but were in fact wrong. Some render that by saying that they were subjectively right but objectively wrong. They did what they thought was right but they made the wrong judgment. We are saying, I suppose, that a wise person—the ideal observer or judge—would not acquiesce in the judgment. Or that an ideal law-maker who made wise laws to lead the community to its flourishing would outlaw such conduct. (We are struggling here with the difference between what is right and *knowing* that something is right.) There will be argument, no doubt, about who is to say that others are in error. But I suppose one would have to allow that if the generality of wise and prudent people thought so, that would be a fair indication; obviously it would not make it wrong but it would be a strong indication. Remember the advice of Aristotle that one should consult the wise person. There is no other way. One could, of course, say that God knows certainly what is right and wrong but how are we to know? God leaves us to find out. What we are saying here is that there *are* right answers to be found—even if they are not easily found.

FREEDOM OF CONSCIENCE

One who seriously believes that a particular course of action is right and obligatory has no option but to follow it and and one who believes that a particular course is permissible is entitled to follow it. One must follow conscience: one may not act against conscience. An action is good which is done in accordance with a sincere conscience even though it deviates from what is objectively right, from what the wise one would say. I am talking about a person who, for whatever reason, is truly convinced, one who has seriously tried to find the truth. There may be negligence in seeking the truth and one who does not seek earnestly fails morally, not being concerned to discover what is fitting or appropriate, not caring sufficiently for the effects of his/her action on others. But I have said that we live and move in the half-light and it is difficult to assess negligence. Many of us are at least half convinced that what we do is legitimate. Kurt Baier's statement sums it up: 'Ought he do the subjectively or the objectively right act? This question can perplex us only because we have no more than a confused understanding of its sense.... If we mean "does thinking that something is one's duty make it so?" the answer is obviously "no". If we mean "does the moral man do what after careful consideration he has worked out to be what he ought to do?" the answer is of course "yes". If it means "should a person who has worked out what he ought to do as carefully and con-scientiously as can be expected be rebuked for acting on his results?" the answer is plainly "no". If it means "is a man ever to be rebuked for doing what he thought he ought to do?" the answer is of course "Yes, sometimes, for he may culpably have failed in his theoretical task." '[3]

We generally refer to this as following one's conscience, as the right of conscience, or the freedom of conscience. It is a right protected by the United Nations Universal Declaration of Human Rights. It is a recognition of the intimacy and profundity of the moral call in us. One who follows conscience is at the most fundamental level one whose choice is for what is right. There is no other option open to the person: he/she chooses the right in the only way he/she can know it. It is easy to see what a violence it would be to force a person to do anything else: it would ask him/her to go against his/her deep desire for goodness, the desire to do what is right. So the Second Vatican Council had weighty words to say about the intimacy or sacredness of conscience. Conscience it says is the most secret core and sanctuary of a person: to obey it is the very dignity of the person; even though it frequently errs from invincible ignorance it does not lose its dignity. (*The Church in the Modern World* n.16). 'It follows that (one) is not to be forced to act in a manner contrary to conscience. Nor, on the other hand, is (one) to be restrained from acting in accordance with conscience' (*Declaration on Religious Freedom* n.3). It was one of the great achievements of the Council that it not only celebrated conscience but explicitly recognized its rights. A

163

hard-won achievement, too, and due to the devoted work of theologians like John Courtney Murray. It went against the bulk of the Roman Catholic tradition which for so long had adopted an 'error has no rights' position. But it was in accord with the developed thought of Thomas Aquinas. He had given some striking examples. He said that it is virtuous to refrain from fornication but that if for some reason a person believes that such abstinence is sinful he/she sins by so abstaining. Again, belief in Christ is good and salutary: but if a person sincerely, though mistakenly, judges it to be evil, he would sin by embracing the Christian faith.[4]

AN INFORMED CONSCIENCE

It was asserted many times in recent controversies that one may follow conscience but only if it is an informed conscience. The dark hint was that an informed conscience is one that accepts the teaching of a bishop or hierarchy, a Roman Congregation or the Pope. That fails to grapple with the fact that there are Catholics who are sometimes genuinely unable to accept the correctness of the teaching put forward by one or other of these authorities. There is no point in saying that this is not possible or that it should not be the case. It is. They are honestly convinced about their position. Where do they stand now with regard to conscience? Are they entitled to follow it or not? One has only to see what Aquinas had to say on matters that are presumably far more serious to recognise that they are.

Informing conscience means bringing to consciousness the relevant available information on a matter and giving due weight to whatever guidance is on offer. One who does that sincerely informs conscience. There are various sources and kinds of guidance. There is the general tradition of our society, roughly summed up in the Ten Commandments. There is the more general Christian tradition that goes beyond that and about which I will have something to say in a few moments. There is Church teaching. The Church has clearly taught on a few issues but they are a few. For the rest of the moral field and particularly for our unique individual decisions we do not get much help from the Church. (There are also issues on which the Church does not seem to have made up its mind.)

In approaching moral decision what one is seeking is truth:

164

that is the only binding force there can be. An authority can make laws but it cannot make something true. The weight to be given to any piece of guidance is in proportion to the likelihood of its being true guidance, and about Church teaching you must discriminate. I doubt if individual bishops would regard their moral pronouncements as authoritative statements of the truth (unless, of course, they are simply repeating some point of Church doctrine). The view of a national hierarchy will obviously carry more weight but it is not clear that they have any distinctive teaching function as such and much would depend on how they arrive at their decisions; it may be that one or two exercise a dominance in one direction or another in theological matters. The unanimous, or near unanimous, freely given view of the bishops of the world would be a striking argument for the truth of a position: the strength of the argument presumably arises from the fact that so many of those to whom the faith of the Church was especially committed had separately and individually discerned this position. But again one would want to know that they had studied the matter carefully and that they had consulted the faithful (especially in something that lies outside their experience).

Then there are instances of the teaching of Roman Congregations, such as the recent document on IVF and the less recent one on sexual ethics. It is hard to see that Roman Congregations in themselves and as such have any teaching mission or authority. The weight they will have will be that of Papal approval and that seems to be of a less stringent order than the direct teaching of a Pope in an encyclical. So let us look at that. There can be different styles of Papal teaching: one thinks of the inspiring teaching of much of the early part of *Humanae Vitae* and of many documents on justice. Such teaching is rather about the general thrust of moral life, about the virtues and goals to be pursued by the Christian. About such there will be little dispute: indeed there have often been suggestions that teaching should be confined to this level of exhortation. It is when it descends to rules and to universal rules at that—as it often does—that problems arise for conscience.

The teaching of the Pope must obviously be treated with great respect: to make little of it is unbecoming a Catholic; it is a failure in the religious obedience enjoined by Vatican II. Not to consider it seriously is a failure to bring an important source of guidance to consciousness. Such teaching however is not infallible: if it were, one would have the absolute certainty of correct guidance, although there might still be argument about its interpretation. But to say that it is not infallible does not mean in any sense that it is erroneous. But it does mean that it could change and that it cannot be given the absolute weight that infallible teaching would merit. (We have to allow also for the fact that the Church finds it difficult to change its position; understandably it will do so only after a very considerable length of time and will err on the side of conservatism. But there are examples of some change in moral matters, as in its teaching on the 'safe period'.) However, there is a strong presumption in favour of Papal teaching and one could only dissent from it for grave reasons. But not all of it can be put in the same category: there may be grave reasons for questioning the wisdom of one part rather than another. Or at least for questioning whether its teaching is to be regarded as a universal rule rather than as an ideal or a rule of high validity that yields to exceptional circumstances (as some hierarchies have interpreted *Humanae Vitae*). Such reasons would be different interpretations coming from hierarchies, serious questions from the theological community (or from the philosophical community in matters of natural law) and above all a widespread inability on the part of the faithful to acknowledge the teaching in its absoluteness (universality) as an obligatory way of Christian life.

One need only read the letter columns of the daily papers at times of controversy to see that there is a deep chasm—a sincerely held difference of opinion—between Catholics on the relation of Church teaching to the formation of conscience. One group will say, 'The Pope/the bishops have said so-and-so': that for them is the end of the affair; they cannot understand how one can be a faithful Catholic or have an informed conscience and not accept that as decisive. The other group is not convinced by the fact that Pope or bishop has spoken: their question is whether what is uttered is necessarily and certainly the right solution to a problem. There is no meeting of minds here. It is well to admit that there are serious questions about some well-known instances of Roman teaching: one thinks of the crucial distinction between 'natural' and 'artificial' birth control, of sterilisation and of IVF in the so-called simple case. Reiteration of the position does not do anything to dispel the difficulty. One can see how a sincere Catholic would have genuine doubts on such issues: there are enough problems about them to make dissent and good faith understandable.

Concentration on a few points of Church teaching, however, may blind us to a more important forming of conscience. There is a danger that we will limit our moral perspective to a few old chestnuts and miss the broad sweep of our responsibilities. It is easy to trundle along with the concerns of an earlier age but there must be development and refinement of our moral sensibilities. That is taking place to some degree. It is not only a matter of detail but of fundamental attitude. We are, I think, slowly becoming aware that the wrongness of immorality is not in disobedience to a rule—even a rule of God— but in a failure of love. Conduct is wrong if and because it involves lack of respect, hardness of heart, antagonism or exploitation of others. Morality seen in this perspective, as we said in treating of the primacy of love, brings a shift of emphasis and perhaps a relativisation of values. It takes courage to see that through, to create a moral climate that is founded on and judged by love. It is not surprising that when that happens one finds people asking, for example, why there is such concern among Church authorities about contraception in marriage and so little about the macho culture, the exploitation of women, and violence in the home. Which is the greater failure: do we need to revise our emphases?

I think we have come also to a dawning awareness of our responsibilities to and our failure towards the marginalised—women generally, the unemployed, the travelling people, the handicapped, the homeless, the foreigner, the prisoner, those from disadvantaged areas. We have moved somewhat from a narrow one-to-one morality to some sense that justice must be done and that it is not done by a preservation of the status quo. The old text book of moral theology defined restitution as the restoration of the balance that had been disturbed by theft or injury as if the status quo with its inequality was just and to be canonised. We realise now that this is not so, that justice must be created by changing situations and above all by changing structures and that this is the responsibility of all of us. We have some slight awareness too of the injustice which we do not only to those near us but to weaker economies and Third World countries. And yet it is difficult to clinch this, difficult for us to take injustice as seriously as other forms of immorality. Much more needs to be done to broaden our perspective and to get the balance right. The Irish bishops produced an excellent document on justice some years ago and many people are still wondering why it made so little impact. Politicians genuinely interested in social reform often wonder why the Churches cannot harness the Christian message to the creation of a political will in favour of the poor and oppressed: we are still predominantly a society that grabs all it can for itself and its sectional interest, that will insist on maintaining the privileged differential of pay. Nothing will happen, I fear,—the shift of consciousness will not take place—until institutionally we are seen to regard greed, injustice and raw competition as being as inimical to the Christian ethos as other forms of immorality. An Irish theologian once asked why it was that there was a press conference in Dublin for *Humanae Vitae* but none for *Populorum Progressio*.

Is there such a thing as a Christian conscience and is conscience the voice of God? Yes, there is such a thing as a Christian conscience, and here we can recall material from earlier chapters. It was what we meant by the 'I' that discerns, by Christian character and imagination. The great story and the many sub-stories that shape the Christian *Gestalt* must be actively present to us. They will form our sensibilities, perspectives and goals, they will give us our preferences and scale of values—if we can allow ourselves to listen. They will modify and shape the central moral terms for us—good, welfare, fulfilment, flourishing. They will colour our feel for the daily issues: hope, trust, disappointment, pain, winning and losing, seeking justice and living with injustice. Informing one's conscience involves all of that for the Christian. It requires, I think, quiet and prayer. We need to put ourselves in context, to let the mud of surface desires settle, to let the kingdom-message invade our hearts and persuade us. Then we might find the truth even of the paradoxes and discontinuities of the Sermon on the Mount—that it is blessed to be poor, meek, merciful, peacemakers and that such is the way to true and full life. There is nothing esoteric about this. Many do it quite spontaneously: the scenes from the life of Jesus, the values which he lived, the crucifix on the wall,have been for many a one the inspiration that lifted them to an extra-ordinary—and tranquil—life of forgiveness, patience and love. Insight is a gift and there is no gift like that of knowing how to live well. There is no wisdom to compare with that.

There is a Christian conscience also in the sense that the total context of decision is religious. Our second chapter considered that. The fundamental awareness of the Christian is of a Creator-God, our beginning and end, Lord of history, God of love, the ultimate horizon of all love and truth and therefore inseparable from all moral effort. So Christian moral life must be lived in this perspective: it is the place where one meets God. It is in this sense that the moral call can be said to be the voice of God. We have seen problems about the model which one has for this—in what sense is morality to be understood as the law of God, for example? So one has to be careful of the kind of God-talk involved. But there is no doubt that for the Christian the whole of moral life assumes a critically different significance: moral responsibility and the exercise of conscience have awesome implications of response to God or rejection of his love. Most Christians know this only too well: it has to be acknowledged that more often than not the religious context of decision-making has been a source of anxiety rather than of joy for Christians. 'The second pain which will afflict the souls of the damned in hell is the pain of conscience. . . . The viper which gnaws the very hearts and core of the wretches in hell. . . .' (James Joyce, *A Portrait of the Artist as a Young Man*).

MORALITY AND LAW

I return to freedom of conscience for a moment. We can be grateful that it has been recognised in this age. But the freedom is not open-ended: there are limits to a person's entitlement to do what he/she thinks right, limits which are often set by State law. C. D. Broad put the matter strikingly: 'There is a very important sense of "ought" in which it is true to say that a person ought always do that alternative which he believes, at the time when he has to act, to be the most right or the least wrong of all those that are open to him. . . . But the more fully this is admitted, the more obvious does the following complementary fact become. The most right or the least wrong act open to other individuals or to a society in certain cases may be to prevent a conscientious individual from doing certain acts which he ought, in this sense, to do, and to try to compel him to do certain acts which he ought, in this sense, to refrain from doing.' The issue arises as that of the relationship of morality and law: I mention it briefly because we have been through much trauma about it in Ireland recently.[5]

How such a constraint on conscience should be interpreted is the problem. It is easy to seize upon it as an excuse for a return to 'error has no rights' or for a simplistic appeal to the common good. It was said in the abortion and divorce referenda debates in this country that the right to follow conscience must bow to the common good, this being identified with what the speaker regards as true or with what his/her Church teaches on a particular point of morality. This is to over-simplify matters: the common good involves among other things seeking ways in which a community can best accommodate different points of view—not the quashing of points of view.

It is difficult for us to break out of the prejudice that our own point of view really is the right one and that in the end others should yield to it. One has to lean over backwards to be just. Seeking genuine accommodation is in a sense trying to function from behind what in another context has been called a veil of ignorance. It is a matter for the community of trying to work out what is the fair or moral thing to do, in a situation in which different sides believe that they are right and in which there is no tribunal to which appeal can be made for a judgment. One has to enter fully into the conviction of the other side that it is right. One has to give as much weight to other positions as to one's own. The judgment to be made is a moral one about the kind of context (set of laws) that is just in this complex situation. In issues of law and morality the aim is not to find the morality of a particular piece of behaviour but to find the moral stance to be taken by the State when people hold different positions sincerely. (That is not the whole of the issue because the question is to be asked not only about those

170

who are in good faith but about those in bad faith, i.e. those who know that their behaviour is wrong. The point is that the law is not the guardian of private morals, that there is a morality that is quite simply not the business of the criminal law. But I am not concerned with that wider issue here in the context of conscience.)

Fortunately the main lines of this issue have been outlined in the famous debate between Professor Hart and Lord Devlin. Roughly it is a matter of how much the law should interfere in moral matters, one side holding that the whole fabric of society is fit matter for the criminal law, the other that the law should interfere minimally and only in order to protect citizens from harm. It seems to me that a Christian may take either side in that debate or some position in between. The issue is one of legal philosophy, of the function and role of the State, and there is nothing in Christian faith to say that the State should interpret its role in one way rather than in the other. It can hardly be stressed too often that it is entirely compatible for a Catholic to hold that a particular kind of behaviour is immoral but that the State should not criminalise it. There is no reason whatever for thinking that those who want the State to criminalise homosexuality or contraception or to ban divorce are more moral or more Christian than those who do not. It may well be that the opposite is the truth.[6]

SIN AND RECONCILIATION

BUT however we try we fail. We all fail and if we deny it that only means that we are not much in touch with ourselves and have an undeveloped moral sense (1 Jn, 1:8). The experience of failure is one of the primordial experiences of life: it is part of the human condition. And it is complex. We resolve and do not persevere, we promise and do not deliver, we think we are converted and find that we are not. We crave affection, we sulk and distance ourselves, we are swamped by passion. We refuse the call of generosity, we close our minds and hearts when inconvenience looms. We compete, we envy and are jealous, we damn with faint praise. We are blindly aggressive and calculatingly malicious. We hate and plan revenge. Frailty, malice, violence and evil-mindedness weigh on us depressingly. They not only take us over as individuals but become institutionalised in groups, communities, cultures. We suspect and exclude English/Irish, Protestant/Catholic, unionist/nationalist, black/white, man/woman, employer/trade unionist. We war and kill not only out of greed and ambition but because of the idolatry of ideas: who are the true followers of Jesus, Mahomet, Wolfe Tone?

Why? What is it about us? Little wonder that the symbolism of evil is one of the most pervasive symbols in human history and that so many of the world's great myths try to deal with it. The great myth of the Judaeo-Christian tradition put it down to what Cardinal Newman called 'some great aboriginal catastrophe', to an original fall or sin. That it says, is why we are weak and sinful today—for myths are not about the then but the now. We have to deal not only with our own frailty: we inherit the scars of the long struggle of human kind to cope with itself and with the Furies which drive it: we bear within us the defeats of our parents and of the dead generations. And in each of us the struggle begins all over again: 'The emotional struggles of mankind were never resolved. The same things were done over and over, with passion, with passionate stupidity, insect-like, the same emotional struggles in daily reality—urge, drive, desire, self-preservation, aggrandisement, the search for happiness, the search for justification, the experience of coming to being and passing away....' (Saul Bellow, *Him with His Foot in His Mouth*). We hear in our own lives the rumbling of the great subterranean forces—instinct, need, urge, desire, longing—which will not let us be, which manifest themselves in a bewildering variety of ways, in violent eruption and in subtle manoeuvre. We make our life's journey to adulthood confusedly, working out the complex of our needs on the environment—wooing it, cajoling, clinging, fearing, separating, fleeing. Our wants tell us that satisfaction—whatever it is that we restlessly seek—will come when we are first, or best, or most powerful, or with most possessions about us, or most loved. We listen to them and so the spiral of striving and seeking goes on. So we find ourselves trapped in the narrow defiles of immediate desires, only half aware of what is going on in us, unable to listen to our whole selves, only dimly aware of the integration which we most deeply desire ('the impossible union of spheres of existence'), without the wisdom which knows what wholeness is and where it lies.

MORAL FAILURE AS ALIENATION

For whatever reason—out of whatever need or fear or desire—we fail. We hurt others: we invest in unjust structures; we let the poor die. We have to live with the pain of that failure. Moral failure is a kind of alienation from ourselves. Because we have our ideals—and we can no more deny them than any other level of our existence. In failure we seem to be cut off from them, from what we might (with caution) call our better self. We experience a split between what we believe we could be and what we have made, between our potential and our actual selves, between what in some sense we most deeply need and what our wants and desires immediately lead us into. So much so that we sometimes ask: how could I have done that? It is

173

failure at this moral level that is often the source of a sense of worthlessness. However one may have succeeded otherwise in life there can be for many people a gnawing doubt that where it counts most—where one is most a person—they have failed and are no good. So that they are in much need of healing and hope.

We are alienated from others. Because that is what moral failure is. The basic issue in life is whether we will be open to others, at least to the extent of respect, fairness and impartiality, or use them as means to our own ends. It may take us time even to see that: we may never have asked ourselves the question, 'What is my basic stance towards life, towards being with others?' It may be only gradually that we discover that we are locked in our selfishness. Much of the great literature of the world is about motive, about the gradual laying bare of a selfishness that invades even our best-looking acts. It is in our inner lives that the real drama of life is and that is why it is such a rich seam for the novelist. It may be only gradually too that we come to discern our responsibilities for others: recent writing on justice and liberation theology has awakened us to the realisation that others are poor because we are rich, that if the poor are not at our table we are always at theirs. We don't want to hear it too much—I don't anyway. It takes too much conversion. The problem, we have said, is in our hearts and affections. The biblical tradition notes this when it lays stress on sin rather than on sins, i.e. on the condition of our hearts (as symbolically the centre of ourselves and our desires), on what it is that we most value and love. It is this that must be changed.

We are alienated from God. There are traditions in which moral failure does not have grave religious implications. But the link between them is a most crucial element of the Christian tradition. To fail in love for the other is to fail in love of God. It is to fail utterly. 'He who says he is in the light and hates his brother is in the darkness still. He who loves his brother abides in the light. . . . ' (1 Jn. 2:9-10). For John, not to recognise the Son or not to love the brethren is to be in the dark; they are so interconnected as to be interchangeable; one cannot have understood who the Son is or who God is if he/she continues to hate. The message of the twenty-fifth chapter of Matthew's Gospel that 'as you did it to one of the least of these my brethren, you did it to me' is not a pretty piece of

174

decoration on the Christian message: it is laying down a foundation-truth. To love others is to love God.

It is not that one loves God and then—in accordance with the will of God—is disposed to do good to the neighbour. It is not that we have been commanded to love the neighbour and do so out of love of God. It is not that the love of God is the motive for love of neighbour. There is even a more radical unity between the two. The explicit love of neighbour *is* the primary act of the love of God: one can love God whom one does not see only by treating one's visible brother or sister lovingly. Not to love others is not to love God. We call it sin. Sin is a religious word: it denotes that moral fault is not just moral fault but fault in relation to God. We fail the Father who, Christians say, is love and source of love and whose love is made visible in Jesus (1 Jn. 3:16; Jn. 3:16), who seeks to pour his love into our hearts by the Spirit and so to make love present in the world. We fail the Son whose mission was to liberate us from selfishness, to overcome the sin of the world and to create a kingdom of peace and reconciliation. We fail the Spirit who would be love in the world through us, whose fruits, if we could remove the blocks to his presence in us, would be 'love, joy, peace, patience, kindness, goodness, faithfulness, gentleness, self-control. . . .' (Gal. 5:22-23).

We fail the Church. The Church is to be the sacrament of the community of the world, it is to be the place which shows forth what communion, freedom, openness and fairness mean, a community that by its presence and its striking sign-value will bring about the reconciliation of all. To the extent that it is not this it is not the true Church and cannot fulfil its mission. 'I do not pray for these only, but also for those who believe in me through their word, that they may all be one . . . so that the world may believe that thou hast sent me.' (Jn. 17:20-21). The union of the members is a condition of the possibility of belief for others and to the extent that we have failed in this we have failed to let the Church be the true Church and so we have failed the world, the kingdom. We add to the problem, we contribute to the sin of the world.

MORTAL SIN

We all fail. But there are degrees: some failures are more alienating from others amd more destructive of community.

The worse they are humanly, the worse they are religiously: the more one offends the brother or sister the more one fails in response to the Triune God and the greater the sin. How can one measure moral failure? One would have to keep two poles in mind: what is done and how, why, and with what commitment it is done. It has been accepted always that judgment about the degree of moral failure depends on the extent to which a person is committed to or involved in the act. It is only people who commit moral fault. It is only about them that we can use the word 'sin'. So it does not make sense to say that a particular type of act—to steal £50—is a serious or mortal sin: types of act do not sin. We have noted in Chapter 6 that there are different 'depths' to acts. Some are surface acts: I may agree with one person that it is a fine day and with the next that it is chilly; I am not greatly concerned one way or the other; I have not invested myself in it very much. There are other acts in which I may be presumed to have invested heavily and which can be said to have meant much to me. They are acts that could be said to come from my centre, from a deep level of what I am as a person. Simple statements like 'I will' in a marriage ceremony can be presumed to mean a lot.

If there can be serious moral fault there can be a serious refusal of our relationship with God: our tradition says that it can be so serious as to be something like a breakdown. All we have to go on, I think, is that there is this possibility. It is part of our tradition's interpretation of the significance of our moral lives in this world. We said in Chapter 2 that for the Judaeo-Christian tradition religion is moral and morality is religious. It is not that God made commandments and prohibitions (sins) and threatened punishment. If anyone could be said to have made morality we have made it. It is a human institution: it arises spontaneously in life; of ourselves we recognise the claim on us to live with others in a way that respects them and creates community. But the Christian knows that morality is more than morality. Desire for moral truth and love is inescapably desire for the One who is ultimate Truth and Love: action in the world for one's brothers and sisters unites one with the God whose purpose is a kingdom of justice and peace.

Immorality is the opposite of that. Christians call it sin. Sin is a this-worldly failure in relation to one's fellow human beings. But such human failure to live in truth and love with others, to become that kind of person, is in effect and whether one adverts to it or not, also a failure to be open to God—'As you did it not to one of the least of these, you did it not to me.' (Mt. 25:45). Sin signifies the religious dimension of moral fault. There is no other sin, no list of sins emanating from God. We must not revert here to a different notion of morality: God does not make sins. There is nothing mysterious about what constitutes the matter of sin: any and every activity which dehumanises qualifies for that. People sometimes ask in fear 'Is such and such a sin?'. If it is an offence against the other or against the community it is: there is no secret list of sins anywhere to which only the clergy have access. It is not a question therefore of God setting us a task. It is a question at root about humanness, about whether we are willing to listen to the call to be whole human beings with others: if we are, we are in union with God and in tune with his purposes.

Our Church tradition holds that some of our inner-worldly failures can be so inhuman as to have the implications of a breach of relationship with God. What would constitute such a grave failure we do not know. We are talking about an act that involves utter and final failure for the individual, that cuts one off from one's destiny, that thwarts all that was planned and purposed by God for his children. Such an act could only be an evil act of the most profound import—a very deep and free decision for badness—and, most likely, a choice that endures as a permanent disposition over time. (Some refer to mortal sin as a state rather than as an act. But it is acts that make states and some acts may be the clinching or definitive commitment to a state.) We must be talking then about someone who is attached to wrongness in the depth of the heart, who has, so to speak, settled for it. (Though this does not mean a formal decision to want wrongness in itself but only to do what involves wrongness.) This means that one cannot commit mortal sin by accident. It is not something that happens to a person: the emphasis is all on choice and on very deep choice at that. We said earlier that one determines oneself, makes up one's mind, engages one's heart, decides one's values, creates one's moral personality or character. It is not easy to change all that, to change one's heart at its centre, to undo all that has been done. So it is of the nature of things that one cannot be hopping in and out of mortal sin: one who seems to be, has either not entered into it or not left it. What matters overall is whether a person has become basically good and decent to others—even though he/she is not able totally to listen to the claim of goodness and indeed does not want to know about it in smaller matters; or basically so engrossed in self, so bad, that no one or nothing—no matter what the cost to others—has been allowed to stand in the way of his/her plans and desires. Theologians sometimes put this by saying that what matters is a person's fundamental option.

The emphasis then, you could say, is not so much on what is done as on the way it is grasped or assented to by a person. Obviously there are superficial actions in our lives—half thought out, half consented to. There are smaller failures—meannesses, unfairness, infidelity, envies, dishonesties, hurts—that do not engage us deeply. We refer to them traditionally as venial sins. These are failures in relation to God, others and self, obstacles to community, problems for the growth of the kingdom. But they are not acts that engage us in our nuclear person, not radical choices of who we want to be. They are superficial enough to be passing comments on life rather than life statements. They are compatible with a general condition of goodness and right relations with others. On the other hand Karl Rahner has the interesting remark that what look like venial sins may be 'the distant echo and summer lightning of a basic egoism which in the end is really mortal'—perhaps indications of a deep depression elsewhere in our moral attitude.[1]

The tradition required three conditions for mortal sin—grave matter, full knowledge and full consent. In practice these were reduced to grave matter: a certain kind of behaviour—a certain sum in matters of justice—was declared to constitute mortal sin. The more we have come to appreciate that matter cannot sin, only people, the more the emphasis has been put on the other two elements. The stress now placed on the depth to which a person commits him/herself to moral wrongness—something that comes from a better psychological understanding of how we act—the stress on badness, is another way of talking about full knowledge and consent. We are more ready to recognise that the fact that someone has performed a certain kind of action is not in itself proof that he/she has committed mortal sin. No one can know for sure when anyone has committed a mortal sin. Nor can we know it even about ourselves. The very best we can have is some kind of presumption. We have to keep in mind the limitations on freedom: we do not know why anybody performed a particular act, what brought him/her to it, with what freedom of choice it was placed. (Remember the remark of St Therese that she expected as much from the justice of God as from his mercy.)

Our Church tradition did list sins as mortal. But just as the Church cannot make behaviour wrong—it does not make morality—neither can it make it seriously wrong. To say that certain kinds of behaviour are mortal sin could only mean that there is a presumption that they are the kind that are likely to engage us in evil in a very radical way—that means in deeply-rooted selfishness and alienation from our fellow human beings. It is proper for a Church to teach and express its view on what kind of behaviour it regards as falling into this category. So the matter or the object of the act remains important. One could of course disagree about whether or not a particular type of behaviour is likely to involve the human being in radical evil in this way: there might be different perceptions of this from age to age, from culture to culture; we have made the point already that factors such as background, status, sex, etc. affect our perceptions of morality and that there is a shifting emphasis in the assessment of moral failure. But whatever about listing types of sin, what matters in the end is whether commitment to wrongness comes from the centre of one's being, from the deepest source of human choice.

The enormity of the implications of mortal sin has led some Roman Catholic theologians to raise questions about an easy classification of sins as mortal. The question is whether what appear to be isolated acts of immorality, let's say of pre-marital sex or contraception, are to be presumed to be mortal. (It is not easy to speak generally about this because there is no knowing what weight a single act carries in the life of any individual.) It has led to an interesting attempt to re-classify sins. The suggestion is that many of the types of act which were traditionally called 'mortal' should be put in a new category of 'serious' sin. It is agreed that they are considerable faults which affect our relationship with others and with God. But they are not to be presumed to carry the consequences of mortal sin.

The suggestion is that the Church's concern for the life of the individual and of the community has led it to require that conduct of this kind be subjected to its rite of reconciliation. The overall concern is clear—to reserve 'mortal' for what is altogether deeper and more abiding, a more rare condition than the easy classification of sins would have led us to believe. One of the curious consolations of human nature may be that just as we find it difficult to give ourselves unreservedly to goodness—there is often some little alloy of selfishness even in our good acts—it may also be that there is some residual love of goodness in us when we do grave wrong. Perhaps it is that which saves us from mortal sin.

Mortal sin is not necessarily a definitive state. A fundamental choice is always reformable: one does not totally dispose of oneself in any one choice. But if it were to become definitive—if utter alienation from our fellow human beings were to become the wholly voluntary decision of our temporal lives—that, our tradition asserts, would result in definitive separation from God. It had colourful ways of conveying that—the fires of hell, etc. The core of the matter, however, is that we can choose in our overall life's decision to be separated from God. Whether human beings do so or have done so, we do not know. When and how—precisely by what kind of life—it is done, we do not know either. What 'death in mortal sin' involves is obviously very difficult to pin down.

What the tradition says is that life is lived over the possibility of this kind of ultimate failure. If we are finally parted from God it is because we choose it as our life's statement. The freedom of the human person to dispose of him/herself is his/her greatness and mystery. Nobody can make us love or value anything or anybody, not even God: this is our most personal and precious right; it is for us to decide who we want to be, where we set our hearts, what we value. Nor can God make us love goodness, love him. Our terrible greatness is that we are free and that willy-nilly we make a life choice. The Christian interpretation is that freedom with regard to the choice of moral goodness is in the end freedom with regard to something much greater—freedom of response to God's gift of himself. We cannot choose to love God directly: we can only choose him 'in the bits and pieces of everyday'; that indeed is how we build our heaven—'as you did it to one of these. . . .' Over time we take up our stance towards the

moral good (towards openness to others or towards selfishness),
we decide what kind of people we want to be, we make our life
choice and in that we determine our salvation or loss. If there is
judgment we judge ourselves. (We are back again here with the
God—morality—salvation model which we mentioned in
Chapter 2.)

RECONCILIATION

Too much concentration on the catastrophic effects of
mortal sin can deflect us from the fact that daily, to some
degree, we are all at odds with one another, that we sow
distrust rather than make community, that we are obstacles to
the love of God in the world. Sometimes seriously so even if
not to the extent of mortal sin. What are we to do with our
persistent failures?—'For I do not do the good I want, but the
evil I do not want is what I do ... who will deliver me from this
body of death?' (Romans 7:19, 24). This seems to me to be an
elemental human and Christian cry. It is the human condition,
a depressing fact that must be faced by every philosophy and it
is caught in a special light by Christianity with its talk of sin, of
the sin of the world, of Christ's struggle to overcome the sin
that is in and among us, that is knotted into the structures that
we make. We stand in continuing need of acceptance and
healing, of reconciliation with others, with God, with
ourselves and with our environment.
The heart of the Christian message is that we can expect
forgiveness—and that it should become a dynamic in our lives.
We may find it difficult to forgive ourselves. Others may find it
difficult to forgive us. History may not forgive us. We may not
be able to undo the harm that we have done. But our story is
that the one whom we regard as the ultimate reality, God, is
forgiving. We may have to live with the tragedies which we
have caused and that is part of our pain. We can only entrust
them to God. We can hope that God's saving presence is still
near to us and to situations of our making which he did not
want (just as we go on hoping in him when our own best efforts
for truth and goodness are thwarted by others). That is not any
kind of explanation or palliative: putting our evil deeds in that
context is not a cheap forgetting of them; they will not be
washed away in their immediate effects on others. But we have

an ultimate context for all things which is beyond what we can see. We say that God can bring good out of evil. If we see at all it is only very darkly: we have never been able to solve the mystery of the inter-relation of that triad of ideas—God, freedom, evil.

But we know that we can expect forgiveness. We know this in Jesus Christ: in him it has been made visible. (1 Jn. 7-9; 1 Jn. 3:16; Jn. 3:16). 'The Scribes and the Pharisees brought a woman who had been caught in adultery, and placing her in the midst they said to Him....."Now in the law Moses commanded us to stone such. What do you say about her?"' The holy law said it. There was a legal justice which told you what to do: there was to be retribution. But Jesus showed a different logic: 'Let him who is without sin among you be the first to throw a stone at her'. Can we afford to engage in legal justice when we have all sinned. There is a closed repetitive logic about such retribution. But there is another perspective that is not determined by the past but that is creative, innovative, risk-taking. It makes space for new initiatives. The woman taken in adultery had come to a dead-end—if the Jews had their way. But Jesus opened up vistas, possibilities, a new life for her.

When we place ourselves before God in our sin—and it is such an important and pervasive experience that our Church has sacramentalised it in rite—what we hear above all is such good news, the story of God's mercy and forgiveness through the ages made visible in Christ. We are inserted into that story. The experience should help to heal us: if God can forgive us can we not understand and have pity on our own weakness, be gentle with ourselves. (That is not enough, of course: we have said earlier that prayer and the sacramental rite do not solve everything, we need the human experience of comfort and counsel—gifts of the Spirit [Rom. 12], equally graces of God.) But the experience of forgiveness is also a challenge. It is an encounter with the disturbing logic of the one who is source and sustainer of all life. It is a glimpse of a new way: we do not have to hate those who hate us or get even with those who wronged us or prove ourselves before those who challenge us or envy those who are better and brighter. 'But I say to you, Love your enemies and pray for those who persecute you, so that you may be sons of your Father who is in heaven; for he makes his sun rise on the evil and on the good, and sends rain on the just and on the unjust. For if you love those who love you. . . . ' (Mt. 5:43ff).

Christianity says that in our darkness there is hope and light. The ground of our being is mercy and love. The overarching symbol of our Christian lives is that of Shepherd/Saviour. We have received mercy: there is hope that we can show mercy. The challenge is to be moved and enabled by the experience of forgiveness to try to exorcise from our lives the animal aggression, the rough justice, the subtle revenge, the crude spiral of violence. The experience of mercy is not a soft option. You have been forgiven, therefore forgive: that is the dynamic. It carries responsibilities. It is to have its effects in the world, in action for forgiveness, peace and reconciliation.

When I refer to reconciliation I am not thinking only of the sacramental rite. There are different moments and rites of reconciliation: sacraments are not always the most significant and fruitful moment for us: the grace of God is bounteously abroad in the world and will not be confined. What does seem to be true is that some awareness of human finitude and frailty is part of the authentic human condition and that some sense of being a sinner before God and others is part of the Christian life. It is to be a permanent disposition with us. It should not be a source of depression but of grateful humility; that is why life can be eucharistic. (It is a pity that we all find it so difficult to acknowledge failure: one of the curious joys of being a Christian, it seems, is to be able to admit it. Some years ago the Brazilian bishops asked pardon for the sins and failings of the Church and it had an electrifying effect.)

The sacramental rite offers special possibilities: it can be a high point. It provides us with a total, rich, body-soul experience of hearing and touching the forgiving love of God (you know how you want to be held, to feel, when someone receives you back). Or it could do so. 'God the Father of mercies through the death and resurrection of his Son has reconciled the world to himself and sent the Holy Spirit among us for the forgiveness of sins'—this is the good news which the priest proclaims in every confession. Unfortunately, the rite of confession in the past has been very much a hole-in-the-wall affair, a place of dark fear. There have been developments but I think it is widely agreed that sacramental reform has been least successful in this area. But it has marvellous possibilities for enabling us to face and integrate in a way that is authentically human and Christian the deep reality of our failures.

One possibility that has emerged is the communal aspect of reconciliation. That is significant. It reminds us that sin is not a private affair between ourselves and God and that the world is not just a stage on which we work out our personal salvation. We sin aginst one another and together, as cliques, classes and cultures, we sin against those whom we regard as rivals or outsiders. Together we are part of sinful humankind, of the sin of the world. It is proper that together as a people we acknowledge that and together receive forgiveness. The communal admission of sin should make for a kindliness—'Let him who is without sin among you....' The communal acceptance of mercy could mark a new beginning with each other. Celebration together could give us new hope for ourselves and our world, could kindle again in us a desire for the bringing about of the kingdom. The hope of God as we proclaim and experience his fidelity and mercy—ever old, ever new—is that we will lift our eyes from this experience to all that is broken, that we will commit ourselves to create community with those near us who have known our bitterness, with those far from us who have suffered from our greed, and even with the whole of a creation that has been the victim of our arrogance and mindlessness. The Church is not the perfect society proud of its righteousness, intolerant of weakness. It is the community of the forgiven who will take on the work of forgiveness, peace and reconciliation.

EPILOGUE

WAITING ON GOD
The Pharisee and the Publican

WHEN I was young I cound not understand all the talk about experience. They told me that life cannot be rushed and that some things only come with time. They said that you learn by experience and that you cannot put an old head on young shoulders. The old dog for the hard road, and a wise old owl when you were in need of counsel. Student productions of Shakespeare, a teacher told us, were all very well but students did not know enough about life to appreciate what they were about. An old musician pronounced that nobody, however technically accomplished, should attempt the later Beethoven piano sonatas until he was thirty. I suspected all of this. I could not understand how this golden wisdom could not be packaged and dispensed to us. Why didn't they simply tell us what they knew and not have us wait? It looked like some last-ditch attempt by an older generation to defend their dwindling territory against the incursions of hungry youth.

About all of this I know a bit more now and it seems to colour my faith. I know now that it takes time—life-time—to learn about being a human being. Because it does, it takes time to learn about the Gospels. You have to let life teach you the questions. It sounds woefully banal to say it but it takes time—life-experience—to learn about God. There is a young person's God and a God for the middle aged. Youth can dare, wants to get on with it, does not see the problems, does not count the cost. The coming of the kingdom awaits its strong arms. Praise God. But who is God for those whom you find saying softly that they haven't the energy they had, or that their memories are failing, or that they are too old to start new things? ('Why should the aged eagle dare?') The kingdom comes within them. They have to settle for acceptance

—accepting themselves and being accepted by others. Being accepted by life, by reality—by God.

In returning and rest you shall be saved;
in quietness and in trust shall be your strength.

(Is.30:15)

It takes time to find not just the answers but the questions. One of the things that used puzzle me at first about the writings of Karl Rahner was his emphasis on God as forgiving. (Another was his preoccupation with death. It is not what I am concerned with here but the connection will not be lost on those who follow my drift.) Take, for example, his short formula of Christian faith: 'God gives himself to man in an act of self-bestowal to be his true consummation, and that too even though it is presupposed in this that man is a sinner, so that this act of self-bestowal entails an attitude of forgiving love.' This says something about the human condition and, because it does, it says something about God. But it takes some life-experience in order to grow into it. Time teaches us that God is not just creator, not just liberator, not just a love that is *sui diffusivum,* but that his mercy is above all his works and ours. Theological statements should ring true to life. Time teaches us that Rahner's does.

I was confirmed about this earlier this year. I sat one night in a mission in Central Africa with a colleague—a student from earlier years. We had been together for a few days' reflection, some twenty of us. The World Service News was over and we were quiet. Then he said from beyond the pool of lamplight: 'You talked quite a bit up there about God as forgiving. I don't remember that you made so much of that when I was a student. Anyway, I wouldn't have understood then: I do now.' I didn't understand then, either. It takes time.

That much is by way of lead-in to the parable of the pharisee and the publican. I don't know much about theories of biblical stories or parables. I hope I am right in thinking that this one can be taken more or less at face value. But I have discovered that even then it depends greatly on where you are and what questions you have to put to the text. (Those in the hermeneutics business have more elegant ways of putting the matter.) When I was younger I presumed that the problem with the pharisee was that he was telling lies or adorning things

186

a bit. But there is no suggestion in the text that he was. Later, accepting that the fellow was telling the truth, I was encouraged to interpret the story as a warning against boasting. Now I see that the issue is more fundamental. The problem with the pharisee was that he had the wrong God. The publican might have got his morals wrong but he had his God right. And that turns out to be more important. He went down to his house justified rather than the other.

I read somewhere—was it in von Balthasar's *Life*?—that St Thérèse said that Jesus would not have spent so much time on the pharisees if they were only one small sect in one small country at one time. We may find that way of putting it naive. She is on surer ground when she goes on to say that we are all pharisees. We are. We seek to justify ourselves before God. (Be a good boy/girl and God will love you. Be converted from your sins and turn to God and he will hear you. There go I *but* for the grace of God.) We have been brought up as Roman Catholics with a merit-God. That is why we need to think more of the story of the pharisee and the publican and allow the implications of it to speak quietly into the clamour of our lives. There is a change, I think, but it is barely perceptible. I recently asked a post-graduate student of theology ('But that was in another country. . . .') what he thought about the Catholic doctrine of merit. He replied that he had never heard of it. I don't know if that says more about his training or about shifts in theology. When I gave him a rough outline of the matter he looked at me with something between disbelief and horror.

Rahner is right. We need to build forgiveness into our very idea of God. When we do, we are not busying ourselves with some fussy decoration of our Christianity. We are asking foundation-questions about the human condition. We are asking who we are and where we come from and what we may hope for. What I know now is that the parable is saying, so much more successfully than Paul did, that we are all sinners and all stand in need of the mercy of God. It is saying that all talk about striving and merit—and some of the talk about conversion and repentance—can lead us astray not only in one tract of theology but in the whole. It can distort our idea of God. We are weak and fallible and selfish and perverse in some proportion. We intend and forget. We promise and do not deliver. We propose and do not pursue. We barely manage to camouflage our pettiness and our touchiness about our little empires. We see creations of delicacy gobbled up by the ravages of passion. The more we know about our motives the more shabby some of them are revealed to be. If we have to get all of that right before God accepts us we are without hope.

They say that symbols and myths about evil are among the most pervasive in world literature. It is not surprising: a sense of weakness and failure (and ultimately of death) are among the most primordial of our experiences. There are other facets to us, of course: this is only the shadow side; this Jack, joke, poor potsherd is immortal diamond. But there *is* this and it could be depressing, if we couldn't meet it. Paul found it depressing and asked to be delivered from it. There is mystery here in this valley where moral striving, failure and forgiveness meet. It is a territory in which some of our storytellers—secular and religious—have made more exciting raids on the inarticulate than has our formal theology. One of the earliest stories is this:

> Now the serpent was more subtle than any other wild creature that the Lord God had made. He said to the woman, 'Did God say, "You shall not eat of any tree of the garden"?' ... She took of its fruit and ate; and she also gave some to her husband and he ate. Then the eyes of both were opened, and they knew that they were naked.... (Gen. 3:1, 6-7)

That is one way of dealing with the reality. Our New Testament story seems to me to face the same issue. It is better, more personal, more hopeful.

> He also told this parable to some who trusted in themselves that they were righteous and despised others: 'Two men went up into the temple to pray, one a pharisee and the other a tax collector. The pharisee stood and prayed thus with himself. 'God, I thank thee that I am not like other men, extortioners, unjust, adulterers, or even like this tax collector. I fast twice a week. I give tithes of all that I get.' But the tax collector, standing far off would not even lift up his eyes to heaven, but beat his breast, saying, 'God, be merciful to me a sinner!' I tell you, this man went down to his house justified rather than the other.... (Lk. 18:10-14).

It so happens that this year I saw three plays within a few weeks each of which in its own way set me thinking further along these lines. I feel carried into a cosmic solidarity in sin by the quiet line of the doctor in *Macbeth*, seeing that troubled lady: 'God, forgive us all.' The great issue came back again as Vanya surveyed the wasteland of his life. ('If only I could wake some still bright morning and feel that life had begun again; that the past was forgotten and had vanished like smoke. Oh, to begin life anew....') There are biblical songs and stories that meet that kind of bleakness with quiet hope. There were awkward echoes, too, in Helmer's unloving judgment (*A Doll's House*) on his wife's loving foolishness—the kind of relentless flaying of weakness that only the spuriously holy can quite muster. It left me wondering about our moral judgments, about the climate of our ministry of forgiveness and about the perfect love that casts out fear. (Father, I missed Mass ... and I'm worried about confessions when I was younger ... and is it a sin to—we all remember our youthful, and not so youthful, anxieties.) One meets priests who find hearing confessions depressing not because it is boring but because of the humiliating scavenging for sin in the rag-bag of the heart over which they have to preside. Most of us were afraid to trust the parables as much as we trusted the rules—although our instincts told us otherwise. If we find ourselves almost redundant in that area, it is not entirely our own fault. A revolt of heart and imagination was required but it was fitful and easily put down.

It sometimes seems to me that some branches of the Protestant tradition are more kindly and gentle than are Roman Catholics. Is there a hardness about us that comes from being assured from youth that we—the Church, of course, not we personally (as if there were a difference!)—have always been in the right, that we have proprietorship of the truth and responsibility for the good? The kindliness comes, perhaps, from a greater admission in their theology of the sinfulness and weakness of human kind. If your theology is constructed on the forgiveness of God, you cannot afford to be judgmental. 'Be kind to one another, tenderhearted, forgiving one another, as God in Christ forgave you' (Eph. 4:32). 'Why do you see the speck that is in your brother's eye, but do not notice the log that is in your own eye?' (Mt. 7:3). 'You shall not wrong a stranger or oppress him, for you were strangers in the land of Egypt' (Ex. 22:21). The forgiveness of God has ethical implications for us.

Ethical life could, indeed, be seen as a response to forgiveness. One of the most inspiring pieces of ethical writing I have read (though it does not set out to be such) is Joachim Jeremias's little piece on the Sermon on the Mount. His point is that if we read the Sermon on its own we have torn it out of its total perspective. Every word of the Sermon, he says, was preceded by something else. It was preceded by the preaching of the kingdom of God: 'You are forgiven, you are a child of God, you belong to the kingdom.' It is as if to every saying of the Sermon (so Jeremias puts it) we are first to supply, 'your sins are forgiven'; therefore, because your sins are forgiven, there now follows, 'While you are still in the way with your opponent, be reconciled to him quickly.' Because 'Your sins are forgiven', there now follows, 'Love your enemies, and pray for those who persecute you' .... And so on. The same dynamic comes across in the story of the wicked servant: 'I forgave you all that debt because you besought me; and should not you have had mercy on your fellow servant as I had mercy on you?' (Mt. 18:32-33). To know who you are before God, warts and all, is a healthy state and if it does not depress it can refine. There is wisdom in Yeats' prayer that his daughter would not be too beautiful.

> For such
> being made beautiful overmuch
> consider beauty a sufficient end,
> Lose natural kindness...In courtesy I'd have her chiefly learned:
> Hearts are not had as a gift but hearts are earned
> By those that are not entirely beautiful ....

I have often pondered on what one might call the problem of the ethical God, on the theological concept of punishment and on (what seems to be closely connected with it) the loss of faith among young people. I have rooted around in the neo-Scholastic manuals which have been a major influence on our catechisms and on our popular religious consciousness. Some of what I have found has been horrific and it is as well that it was tempered by a more benign devotional writing and pastoral practice. Take this paraphrase of the very influential moral philosopher, Cathrein. Law, he says (as does almost every other philosopher and theologian of the period) requires a sanction: if God wished his moral law to be kept the only way for him to do it was to impose reward and punishment for it; only the eternal punishment of hell or reward of heaven would be a sufficient stimulus; to impose a lesser punishment would be contrary to the wisdom of God. It would be hard to over-estimate the influence which that has had on our idea of God. It has largely created the Roman Catholic subconscious. It is at the root of our most basic fears and hopes and expectations. It *is* many people's conception of God. Why didn't someone sprinkle in even a pinch of the Aquinas who says that there is no hope of justification in the commandments as such, but in faith alone (In 1 Tim. lect. 3)?

I have wandered into dangerous terrain—justification, no less—and some forward scout of orthodoxy may well pick me off. However, as I said, one can record some thaw in this theology of deterrence. One finds theologians trying to right the picture, saying that faith does not imply a religious perfor-mance by which one attempts to please God but an abandon-ment of any performance on man's part and an admission that he can do nothing himself (Böckle). Or that the purpose for which man must discern good and evil and govern himself is not to secure God's welcome, which is assured him in any case (Burtchaell). Not to mention Küng's major contribution and Rahner's large agreement with him. The roll-call is simply to give some kind of—well, if not theological justification, at least some backing—to my tentativeness here and to what I know is the instinct of others.

What I am trying to point up is that we are to identify ourselves as a community of those who are by definition weak and failing and who acknowledge and accept one another as such. ('I confess to Almighty God . . . and to you, my brothers and sisters, that I have sinned . . . And I ask blessed Mary ever virgin . . . and you, my brothers and sisters, to pray for me . . . .') People who know that they have been accepted by God as such. The glory of us is that we believe together that the ultimate reality is forgiving. We may not be able to forgive ourselves, others may not forgive us, history may not forgive us. But God does—and not conditionally. It is not only if we have first shined and combed ourselves and put on our best suits and made ourselves respectable enough to appear in his presence that he does so. He does it anyway. The ultimate sin, as the parable tells us, is to think that you are somebody, to trust yourself, to count up, to confuse Christianity with knowing that you have done right. Everything is gift and grace and acceptance. It could be that we would never learn that. It is a hard saying of Jesus to those who sit on the chair of Moses that the harlots are nearer to the kingdom than they are. We are never nearer to the kingdom than when together, prelate and pensioner, we recognize that we are all in need of acceptance and forgiveness, that we have received it and that this is cause for common celebration. I don't think we have enough of it in the Church, although the reform of the rite of penance is slowly inching towards it. 'God, have mercy on Bartley's soul and on Michael's soul and on the souls of Shamus and Patch and on Stephen and Shaun and may he have mercy on my soul, Nora, and on the soul of every one is left living in this world.' (J. M. Synge, *Riders to the Sea*).

'Has no man condemned you, woman?' (No man is in a position to condemn when his own sins are written on the ground.) 'Neither will I.' Jesus gets things into focus for that little Gospel group. He did not accuse anyone. He simply let them remember together their humanity and their shared condition before God. That was enough to induce some reticence and to make an unloving zeal for the law look foolish. Jesus had a way of subverting received ideas. You won't get me wrong, I know. I am not making a pitch for bigger and better sins. On the contrary: 'Your sins are forgiven', therefore 'while you are still in the way with your opponent . . . .' What I say is not meant to be depressing but liberating. I am trying to feel my way about God and loving-mercy (*hesed*) and about the gentleness and freedom that come from a common recognition of our flawed beauty. I am concerned about the remark of Vatican II that we are sometimes responsible for the atheism of others. I am wondering about the image of the Church and about signs of credibility:

> For I will leave in the midst of you a people humble and
> lowly.
> They shall seek refuge in the name of the Lord . . .
> For they shall pasture and lie down
> and none shall make them afraid (Zeph. 3:12-13).

I am chewing over: 'For by grace you have been saved

through faith; and this is not your own doing; it is the gift of God—not because of works, lest any man should boast' (Eph. 2:8-9). As I said, there is mystery here and I have not got my theological act fully together. I don't think anyone can. We have so many stories about God, so many skeins of our tribal heritage—not to be worked into some neat and easy pattern. I am only saying that we should dwell on this one more and tell it oftener around the firesides of our hearts. It is a simple tale but it cracks open fundamental issues for us. It was the one who recognized his limitations and failures who went down to his house justified rather than the other (who told no lie but who either had not lived long enough or had not learned much from life). In the end, it is more important for us to get it right with the publican than with the pharisee. We are to wait on the Lord and count on his word. We are to remember that:

> 'Sin must needs be. But all shall be well, and all shall be well, and all manner of thing shall be well' (Julian of Norwich).

That, as they say, is the bottom line for us.

Epilogue appeared in *The Furrow* of January 1983 as part of a series entitled 'The New Testament as Personal Reading'. It is in a rather different style but I have left it unchanged. It may help to put the rest of the book in context. I thank the editor for permission to use it here.

NOTES

Introduction (pp. 1-5)
1. I use the masculine pronoun throughout to refer to God. It indicates—I hope—more a failure to solve the problem of an adequate God-language than the taking of a position on the issue.

Chapter 2 (pp. 23-42)
1. J. Wach, *The Comparative Study of Religions*, New York, 1958, p. 76.
2. B. Williams, *Morality: an Introduction to Ethics*, Penguin, 1972, p. 85.
3. K. Rahner, *Theological Investigations* (trans. K. and B. Kruger), London, 1969, v. 6. p. 215.
4. K. Rahner, *Theological Investigations*, v. 2. p. 272, v. 6, p. 178ff, 242ff.
5. Cf. V. MacNamara, *Faith and Ethics*, Dublin and Washington, 1985, Chapter 7.
6. Thomas Aquinas, in commentary on 2 Cor. 3.

Chapter 3 (pp. 43-61)
1. Cf. *Faith and Ethics*, Chapter 3 for a more detailed discussion.

Chapter 4 (pp. 62-85)
1. C. S. Lewis, *The Four Loves*, London, 1960.
2. Cf. A. Nygren, *Agape and Eros*, London, 1957; G. Gilleman, *The Primacy of Charity in Moral Theology*, London, 1959; M. D'Arcy, *The Mind and Heart of Love*, London, 1946.
3. G. Outka, *Agape: an Ethical Analysis*, New Haven and London, 1972; Cf. K. Rahner, 'What we call the absolute, unqualified validity of moral values is essentially based on the absolute value and absolute dignity of the spiritual and free person.... The human person by its nature and dignity demands an unconditional respect.'; *Theological Investigations*, v. 2, p. 245.
4. Cf. J. A. T. Robinson, *Christian Morals Today*, London, 1964, and *Honest to God*, London, 1963; J. Fletcher, *Situation Ethics*, London, 1966.

194

Chapter 5 (pp 86-109)
1. Thomas Aquinas, *S. Theol.* 1-11, q. 106; in comm. 2 Cor 3.
2. J. Fuchs, *Christian Ethics in a Secular Arena,* Dublin and Washington, 1984, p. 82.
3. These are all terms which appear in official documents. Cf. *Casti Connubii;* Pius XII's Address to Italian Housewives, 29/10/1951; *Humanae Vitae,* n. 16.
4. I have taken this summary from R. McCormick, *How Brave a New World,* London, 1981, p. 5.
5. Cf. especially G. Grisez, *The Way of the Lord Jesus,* (Vol. 1, *Christian Moral Principles)* Chicago, 1983, J. Finnis, *Natural Law and Natural Rights,* Oxford, 1980 and *Fundamentals of Ethics,* Oxford, 1983.

Chapter 6 (pp. 110-130)
1. I. Murdoch, *The Sovereignty of Good,* London, 1970, p. 84.
2. Thomas Aquinas, in comm. 2 Cor 3.
3. For a more detailed examination of motive cf. *Faith and Ethics,* Chapter 4.

Chapter 7 (pp. 131-153)
1. P. Foot, 'The Problem of Abortion and the Doctrine of the Double Effect' in J. Rachels, *Moral Problems,* New York, 1971, p. 40.
2. *The Tablet,* 17/10/87.

Chapter 8 (pp. 154-171)
1. For a detailed discussion cf. J. Glaser, 'Conscience and Superego: a Key Distinction' in C. Ellis Nelson, *Conscience: Theological and Psychological Perspectives,* New York, 1973.
2. I. Murdoch, *The Sovereignty of Good,* p. 67.
3. K. Baier, *The Moral Point of View,* New York, 1958, p. 146
4. *Summa Theol.*, I-II, q. 19, a. 5.
5. C. D. Broad, 'Conscience and Conscientiousness' in J. Donnelly and L. Lyons (eds), *Conscience,* New York, 1973.
6. Cf. V. MacNamara, 'Law and Morality', *The Furrow* 1979, pp. 675ff., 'Morality and Law: Experience and Prospects', *Studies,* Winter 1985, pp. 373ff.

Chapter 9 (pp. 172-184)
1. K. Rahner, *Theological Investigations,* v 6, p. 218.